W9-CVW-789

JOHN DEWEY: DICTIONARY OF EDUCATION

JOHN DEWEY:

DICTIONARY
OF
EDUCATION

Edited by Ralph B. Winn

With a Foreword by John Herman Randall, Jr.

GREENWOOD PRESS, PUBLISHERS
WESTPORT, CONNECTICUT

Library of Congress Cataloging in Publication Data

Dewey, John, 1859-1952.
  Dictionary of education.

  1. Education--Dictionaries. I. Title.
LB875.D37 1972   370'.3   72-139129
ISBN 0-8371-5745-5

Originally published in 1959 by the Philosophical Library,
New York.

Reprinted with the permission of the Philosophical Library.

Reprinted in 1972 by Greenwood Press,
A division of Congressional Information Service, Inc.
88 Post Road West, Westport, Connecticut 06881

Library of Congress catalog card number 72-139129
ISBN 0-8371-5745-5

Printed in the United States of America

10 9 8 7 6 5 4

Foreword

John Dewey was essentially a critic. He was a critic not merely, and not primarily, of the inherited problems of professional and technical philosophers. He was a critic in the grand style. He directed his analysis to what he called in contrast "the problems of men." And by this he meant the entire range of intellectual issues raised by the culture in which he found himself living. He saw emerging our twentieth-century world—a scientific, technological, international world, in which the immense achievement of the cooperative activity of men in groups hangs precariously on the shifting tensions and antagonisms generated between those groups. On all the ideas and problems involved in these complex difficulties, Dewey had something to say, usually novel, and always significant.

Dewey was seeing many things in new relations, and attempting to express original insights. He would try again and again to make his meaning clear, putting his thought now in this form and now in that. In his many pages it is not easy to find the most revealing formulation. A compilation like Dr. Winn's, where the most penetrating and suggestive statements have been carefully singled out and classified, can be of immense help, both to the reader manfully making his way through Dewey's arguments, and to the man who wants ready access to Dewey's most incisive thought on crucial points.

Dewey is not reputed a great stylist, like William James. He did not strike off vivid metaphors that stick in the memory, but often leave their application and precise meaning in dispute. In his writing, as in his teaching before a class, he is primarily a man thinking things out, thinking his way through a problem—trying desperately to get it clear in his own mind, to follow out its leads and its bearings on other problems. He will take an idea, hold it up, look at it from different sides, put it together with another idea, view them both in a fresh light, follow out the new train of thought that suggests. Then he will come back to the first idea for a further look and another start. All the while he is talking and commenting on what he is doing and finding out. The reader, like the class earlier, is privileged to overhear this talk—the revealing talk of a shrewd and penetrating mind thinking aloud.

But every so often the reader is brought up with a start. Dewey sums up a long argument with pithy, well chosen words that make everything fall into place. Sometimes it is an apt illustration that clinches his point. Sometimes it is the putting of a problem in a new way that sticks in the memory. Sometimes it is a statement deliberately provocative that sets one to think furiously. Usually in it Dewey abandons the technical terms of the professional and speaks in the language of everyday. At times he falls back on the homespun words of his Vermont forebears or on the vivid American speech of his young manhood in the Midwest. The effect is electric. Here is intelligence speaking significantly to the problem of men.

For Dewey is a master of the pithy saying, of compressed incisive thought. These apothegms are too full of suggestion and wisdom to be left buried in the discursive pages in which they are embedded. Dr. Winn has had the brilliant idea to select many of the best and let them stand on their own feet. And his success reveals how well Dewey lends himself to such a culling. The Dewey who punctuates his reasoned arguments with these effective sayings is not the whole Dewey, of course. The serious reader will want to go on to explore passages of analysis of which these concentrated statements are the climax, and, to use Dewey's own term, the "consummation." But the skill of Dr. Winn does make clear that John Dewey can rank with the best of those whose wisdom has produced the literature of "philosophical thoughts." When he has brought his explorations and inquiries to a conclusion, Dewey can write, and write brilliantly.

JOHN HERMAN RANDALL, JR.

Columbia University

ACKNOWLEDGMENT

The editor makes grateful acknowledgment to the following publishers and publications for permission to reprint from the works
cited:

The American Teacher: "Crisis in Education" by John Dewey.
Antioch Review: "Democratic Faith and Education" by John Dewey.
Appleton-Century-Crofts, Inc.: *The Educational Frontier* edited by
William H. Kilpatrick, copyright, 1933, The Century Co., re-
printed by permission of Appleton-Century-Crofts, Inc.
Beacon Press, Inc.: *Knowing and the Known* by John Dewey and
A. F. Bentley; and *Reconstruction in Philosophy* by John Dewey.
Columbia University Press: *Construction and Criticism* by John
Dewey; and *Naturalism and the Human Spirit* by Y. H. Krikor-
ian.
Commentary: "Liberating the Social Scientist" by John Dewey.
E. P. Dutton & Co., Inc.: *Schools of Tomorrow* by John and Evelyn
Dewey.
Fortune Magazine: "Challenge to Liberal Thought" by John Dewey.
Harcourt, Brace and Company: *Recent Gains in American Civilization*
edited by Kirby Page.
Harper & Brothers: *Psychology* by John Dewey.
Harvard University Press: *Authority and the Individual.*
D. C. Heath and Company: *How We Think* by John Dewey.
Henry Holt and Company, Inc.: *The Philosophy of John Dewey* edited
by Joseph Ratner.
Houghton Mifflin Company: *Interest and Effort in Education* and
Moral Principles in Education by John Dewey.
The Humanist, published by the American Humanist Association, Yel-
low Springs, Ohio: "Man and Mathematics" by John Dewey.

A

ABSTRACTION

1. Abstraction is indispensable if one experience is to be applicable to other experiences. Every concrete experience in its totality is unique; it is itself, non-reduplicable. Taken in its full concreteness, it yields no instruction, it throws no light. What is called abstraction means that some phase of it is selected for the sake of the aid it gives in grasping something else. Taken by itself, it is a mangled fragment, a poor substitute for the living whole from which it is extracted. But viewed teleologically or practically, it represents the only way in which one experience can be made of any value for another. . . Looked at functionally, not structurally or statically, abstraction means that something has been released from one experience for transfer to another.—*Reconstruction in Philosophy*.

2. There is no science without abstraction and abstraction means fundamentally that certain occurrences are removed from the dimension of familiar practical experience into that of reflective or theoretical inquiry.—*Sources of a Science of Education*.

3. Something of the nature of abstraction is found in the case of all ideas and of all theories. Abstraction from assured and certain existential reference belongs to every suggestion of a

possible solution; otherwise inquiry comes to an end and positive assertion takes its place.—*Knowing and the Known*.

See also: Liberalism 4; School 5; Theory 4.

ACTION

1. We cannot seek or attain health, wealth, learning, justice, or kindness in general. Action is always specific, concrete, individualized, unique.—*Reconstruction in Philosophy*.

2. Action is at the heart of ideas.—*The Quest for Certainty*.

3. No mode of action can, as we have insisted, give anything approaching absolute certitude; it provides insurance but not assurance. Doing is always subject to peril, to the danger of frustration.—*Ibid*.

See also: Aims and Purposes 2; Belief 1; Democracy 3; Experience 1; Knowledge 5, 10; Liberty 4; Philosophy 3; Responsibility 1; Self 3; Theory 3; Understanding 4.

AIMS AND PURPOSES

1. An aim denotes the result of any natural process brought to consciousness and made a factor in determining present observation and choice of ways of acting. It signifies that an activity has become intelligent. Specifically it means foresight of the alternative consequences attendant upon acting in a given situation in different ways, and the use of what is anticipated to direct observation and experiment. A true aim is thus opposed at every point to an aim which is imposed upon a process of action from without. The latter is fixed and rigid; it is not a stimulus to intelligence in the given situation, but is an externally dictated order to do such and such things. Instead of connecting directly with present activities, it is remote, divorced from the means by which it is to be reached. Instead of suggesting a freer and better balanced activity, it is a limit set to activity. In education, the currency of these externally

imposed aims is responsible for the emphasis put upon the notion of preparation for a remote future and for rendering the work of both teacher and pupil mechanical and slavish.—*Democracy and Education.*

2. All purpose is selective, and all intelligent action includes deliberate choice.—*A Common Faith.*

3. Purposes exercise determining power in human conduct. The aims of philanthropists, of Florence Nightingale, of Howard, of Wilberforce, of Peabody, have not been idle dreams. They have modified institutions. Aims, ideals do not exist simply in "mind;" they exist in character, in personality and action. One might call the roll of artists, intellectual inquirers, parents, friends, citizens who are neighbors, to show that purposes exist in an operative way.—*Ibid.*

See also: Desire 3; Education 5, 15; Facts 2; Nature 2; Reason 2; Society 2; Theory 2; Thinking 11.

ART

1. Works of art are the only media of complete and unhindered communication between man and man that can occur in the world full of gulfs and walls that limit community of experience.—*Art as Experience.*

2. Because objects of art are expressive, they are a language. Rather they are many languages. For each art has its own medium and that medium is especially fitted for one kind of communication. Each medium says something that cannot be uttered as well and as completely in any other tongue.—*Ibid.*

3. The arts which today have most vitality for the average person are things he does not take to be arts: for instance, the movie, jazzed music, the comic strip, and, too frequently, newspaper accounts of love-nests, murders, and exploits of bandits. For, when what he knows as art is relegated to the museum and gallery, the unconquerable impulse towards experiences enjoy-

3

able in themselves finds such outlet as the daily environment provides. Many a person who protests against the museum conception of art, still shares the fallacy from which the conception springs. For the popular notion comes from a separation of art from the objects and scenes of ordinary experience that many theorists and critics pride themselves upon holding and even elaborating.—*Ibid.*

4. There must be historic reasons for the rise of the compartmental conception of fine art. Our present museums and galleries to which works of fine art are removed and stored illustrate some of the causes that have operated to segregate art instead of finding it an attendant of temple, forum, and other forms of associated life. An instructive history of modern art could be written in terms of the formation of the distinctively modern institutions of museum and exhibition gallery. I may point to a few outstanding facts. Most European museums are, among other things, memorials of the rise of nationalism and imperialism. Every capital must have its own museum of painting, sculpture, etc., devoted in part to exhibiting the greatness of its artistic past, and in other part, to exhibiting the loot gathered by its monarchs in conquest of other nations; for instance, the accumulations of the spoils of Napoleon that are in the Louvre. They testify to the connection between the modern segregation of art and nationalism and militarism.—*Art as Experience.*

5. A work of art no matter how old and classic is actually, not just potentially, a work of art only when it lives in some individualized experience. As a piece of parchment, of marble, of canvas, it remains self-identical throughout the ages. But as a work of art, it is recreated every time it is esthetically experienced.—*Ibid.*

6. There is a conflict artists themselves undergo that is instructive as to the nature of imaginative experience. . . It concerns the opposition between inner and outer vision. There is a stage in which the inner vision seems much richer and

finer than any outer manifestation. It has a vast, an enticing aura of implications that are lacking in the object of external vision. It seems to grasp much more than the latter conveys. Then there comes a reaction; the matter of the inner vision seems wraith-like compared with the solidity and energy of the presented scene. The object is felt to say something succinctly and forcibly that the inner vision reports vaguely, in diffuse feeling rather than organically. The artist is driven to submit himself in humility to the discipline of the objective vision. But the inner vision is not cast out. It remains as the organ by which outer vision is controlled, and it takes on structure as the latter is absorbed within it. The interaction of the two modes of vision is imagination; as imagination takes form the work of art is born.—*Ibid.*

7. We lay hold of the full import of a work of art only as we go through in our own vital processes the processes the artist went through in producing the work. It is the critic's privilege to share in the promotion of this active process.—*Art as Experience.*

See also: Culture 2; Logic 1; Mind 1; Possibility 2, 3; Science 5; Soul.

AUTHORITY

1. The genuine problem is the relation between authority and freedom. . . . Authority stands for stability of social organization by means of which direction and support are given to individuals while individual freedom stands for the forces by which change is intentionally brought about. The issue that requires constant attention is the intimate and organic union of the two things: of authority and freedom, of stability and change.—"Authority and Social Change," in *Authority and the Individual* (a Symposium).

2. A survey of history shows that while the individualistic

philosophy was wrong in setting authority and freedom, stability and change, in opposition to one another, it was justified in finding the organized institutional embodiments of authority so external to the new wants and purposes that were stirring as to be in fact oppressive. The persons and classes who exercised the power that comes from the possession of authority were hostile to the variable and fresh qualities, the qualities of initiative, invention, and enterprise, in which change roots. The power exercised was the more oppressive and obstructive because it was not just physical but had that hold upon imagination, emotions, and purpose which properly belongs to the principle of authority. Underneath, it was not a conflict between social organization and individuals, between authority and freedom, but between conservative factors in the very make-up of individuals—factors that had the strength that is derived from the inertia of customs and traditions ingrained by long endurance—and the liberating, the variable and innovating factors in the constitution of individuals. It was a struggle for authoritative power between the old and the new; between forces concerned with conservation of values that the past had produced and forces that made for new beliefs and new modes of human association. It was also the struggle between groups and classes of individuals—between those who were enjoying the advantages that spring from possession of power to which authoritative right accrues, and individuals who found themselves excluded from the powers and enjoyments to which they felt themselves entitled. The necessity of adjusting the old and the new, of harmonizing the stability that comes from conserving the established with the variability that springs from the emergence of new needs and efforts of individuals—this necessity is inherent in, or a part of, the very texture of life. —*Ibid.*

3. We need an authority that, unlike the older forms in which it operated, is capable of directing and utilizing change, and

we need a kind of individual freedom . . . that is general and shared and that has the backing and guidance of socially organized authoritative control.—*Ibid.*

4. The need for authority is a constant need of man. For it is the need for principles that are both stable enough and flexible enough to give direction to the processes of living in its vicissitudes and uncertainties. Libertarians have often weakened their case by the virtual assumption that authority in every form and mode is the great enemy. In making this assumption, they play directly into the hands of those who insist upon the necessity of some external and dogmatic authority, whether ecclesiastical or political or a mixture of both. The underlying problem of recent centuries is the question of whether and how scientific method, which is the method of intelligence in experimental action, can provide the authority that earlier centuries sought in fixed dogmas. The conflict of science and religion is one phase of this conflict.—*Problems of Men.*

See also: Belief 2; Democracy 3, 7; Freedom 5; Leadership; Right 1; School 2.

B

BELIEF

1. Any belief as such is tentative, hypothetical; it is not just to be acted upon, but is to be framed with reference to its office as a guide to action. Consequently, it should be the last thing in the world to be picked up casually and then clung to rigidly.—*The Quest for Certainty.*

2. Beliefs current in morals, politics and religion are marked by dread of change and by the feeling that order and regulative authority can be had only through reference to fixed standards accepted as finalities, because referring to fixed antecedent realities. Outside of physical inquiry, we shy from problems; we dislike uncovering serious difficulties in their full depth and reach; we prefer to accept what is and muddle through.—*Ibid.*

3. There is no belief so settled as not to be exposed to further inquiry.—*Logic: the Theory of Inquiry.*

4. During periods in which social customs were static, when isolation of groups from one another was the rule, it was comparatively easy for men to live in complacent assurance as to the finality of their own practices and beliefs. That time has gone. The problem of attaining mutual understanding and a reasonable degree of amicable cooperation among different peoples, races, and classes is bound up with the problem of

reaching by peaceful and democratic means some workable adjustment of the values, standards, and ends which are now in a state of conflict.—"Antinaturalism in Extremis," in *Naturalism and the Human Spirit* (a Symposium, ed. by Y. H. Krikorian).

See also: Children 2; Desire; Experimental Method 1, 2; Logic; Loyalty 2; Religion 2, 7, 9.

BRAIN

The brain is primarily an organ of a certain kind of behavior, not of knowing the world.—In the *Creative Intelligence*: Essays in the Pragmatic Attitude (a Symposium).

See also: Environment 5; Man 3; Self 4; Thinking 9.

C

CAUSE AND EFFECT

1. The first thinker who proclaimed that every event is effect of something and cause of something else, that every particular existence is both conditioned and condition, merely put into words the procedure of the workman.—*Experience and Nature*.

2. A "cause" is not merely an antecedent; it is that antecedent which if manipulated regulates the occurrence of the consequent. That is why the sun rather than night is the causal condition of day.—*Ibid*.

See also: Chance.

CERTAINTY

1. Men readily persuade themselves that they are devoted to intellectual certainty for its own sake. Actually they want it because of its bearing on safeguarding what they desire and esteem.—*The Quest for Certainty*.

2. The quest for certainty is a quest for a peace which is assured.—*Ibid*.

See also: Action 3; Chance.

CHANCE

Man finds himself living in an aleatory world; his existence involves, to put it baldly, a gamble. The world is a scene of risk; it is uncertain, unstable, uncannily unstable. Its dangers are irregular, inconsistent, not to be counted upon as to their times and seasons. . . Our magical safeguard against the uncertain character of the world is to deny the existence of chance, to mumble universal and necessary law, the ubiquity of cause and effect, the uniformity of nature, universal progress, and the inherent rationality of the universe. Those magic formulae borrow their potency from conditions that are not magical. Through science we have secured a degree of power of prediction and control. . . But when all is said and done, the fundamentally hazardous character of the world is not seriously modified, much less eliminated.—*Experience and Nature.*

See also: Law of Nature 3; Security 1.

CHANGE

1. Since changes are going on anyway, the great thing is to learn enough about them so that we be able to lay hold of them and turn them in the direction of our desires. Conditions and events are neither to be fled from nor passively acquiesced in; they are to be utilized and directed. They are either obstacles to our ends or else means for their accomplishment.—*Reconstruction in Philosophy.*

2. Whatever influences the changes of other things is itself changed.—*Experience and Nature.*

3. Today there are no patterns sufficiently enduring to provide anything stable in which to acquiesce, and there is no material out of which to frame final and all-inclusive ends. There is, on the other hand, such constant change that acquiescence is but a series of interrupted spasms, and the outcome is mere drifting. In such a situation, fixed and comprehensive goals are but irrelevant dreams, while acquiescence is not a policy but its abnegation.—*Individualism, Old and New.*

4. It is demonstrable that many of the obstacles to change

which have been attributed to human nature are in fact due to the inertia of institutions and to the voluntary desire of powerful classes to maintain the existing states.—"Human Nature," in the *Encyclopedia of the Social Sciences*, VII.

5. Any existential change is from a past into a present, something future to its past.—Reply in *The Philosophy of John Dewey* (a Symposium, ed. by P. A. Schilpp).

See also: Authority 1, 3; Belief 2; Conservatism 2, 4; Experience 1; Experimental Method 2; History 6; Knowledge 6; Law 2; Liberalism 4; Morality 7; Nature 1.

CHARACTER

1. A man may give himself away in a look or a gesture. Character can be read through the medium of individual acts. —*Human Nature and Conduct*.

2. Character is the interpenetration of habits. If each habit existed in an insulated compartment and operated without affecting or being affected by others, character would not exist. That is, conduct would lack unity being only a juxtaposition of disconnected reactions to separate situations.—*Ibid.*

See also: Aims and Purposes 3; Interaction 2; Responsibility 3; School 8; Society 4.

CHILDREN

1. Children's alleged native egoism is simply an egoism which runs counter to an adult's egoism. To a grown-up person who is too absorbed in his own affairs to take an interest in children's affairs, children doubtless seem unreasonably engrossed in their own affairs.—*Democracy and Education*.

2. Because of his physical dependence and impotency, the contacts of the little child with nature are mediated by other persons. Mother and nurse, father and older children determine what experiences the child shall have; they constantly instruct

him as to the meaning of what he does and undergoes. The conceptions that are socially current and important become the child's principles of interpretation and estimation long before he attains to personal and deliberate control of conduct. Things come to him clothed in language, not in physical nakedness, and this garb of communication makes him a sharer in the beliefs of those about him.—*Reconstruction in Philosophy.*

See also: Education 8, 9; Learning 1; Obedience; Reading; School 1, 5; Teaching 1, 6.

CHOICE

Intelligent choice is still choice. It still involves preference for one kind of end rather than another one which might have been worked for. It involves a conviction that such and such an end is valuable, worthwhile, rather than another.—In *The Educational Frontier* (with J. L. Childs; a Symposium, ed. by W. H. Kilpatrick).

See also: Aims and Purposes 1, 2; Individuality 2; Self 2, 3.

CIVILIZATION

1. If ever there was a house of civilization divided within itself and against itself, it is our own today.—"A Critique of American Civilization," in *Recent Gains of American Civilization* (a Symposium, ed. by K. Page).

2. Our civilization is so predominantly a business civilization.—*Individualism, Old and New.*

3. The measure of civilization is the degree in which the method of cooperative intelligence replaces the method of brute conflict.—*Liberalism and Social Action.*

4. We are living in a mixed and divided life. We are pulled in opposite directions. We have not as yet a philosophy that is modern in other than a chronological sense. We do not have as yet an educational or any other institution that is not a mixture

of opposite elements. Division between methods and conclusions in natural science and those prevailing in morals and religion is a serious matter, from whatever angle it be regarded. It means a society that is not unified in its most important concerns.—"Challenge to Liberal Thought," in the *Fortune*, XXX (1944).

5. Civilization itself is the product of altered human nature. —*Problems of Men*.

See also: Education 1, 11; Humanity; Individual 1; Language 2; Learning 2; Philosophers 5.

CLASSIFICATION

Things have to be sorted out and arranged so that their grouping will promote successful action for ends. . . Classification transforms a wilderness of byways in experience into a well-ordered system of roads, promoting transportation and communication in inquiry.—*Reconstruction in Philosophy*.

COMMUNICATION

Communication is a process of sharing experience till it becomes a common possession.—*Democracy and Education*.

See also: Art 1, 2; Children 2; Classification; Community 1; Discussion 1; Freedom of Thought 2; Words 3, 4.

COMMUNITY

1. Men live in a community in virtue of the things which they have in common; and communication is the way in which they come to possess things in common. What they must have in common in order to form a community or society are aims, beliefs, aspirations, knowledge—a common understanding—like-mindedness as the sociologists say. Such things cannot be passed physically from one to another, like bricks; they cannot be shared as persons would share a pie by dividing it into physi-

cal pieces. The communication which insures participation in a common understanding is one which secures similar emotional and intellectual dispositions—like ways of responding to expectations and requirements.—*Democracy and Education.*

2. As soon as a community depends to any considerable extent upon what lies beyond its own territory and its own immediate generation, it must rely upon the set agency of schools to insure adequate transmission of all its resource.—*Ibid.*

See also: Conscience; Democracy 5; Education 5; Humanity; Justice; Philosophy 6; State 4.

CONDUCT

All conduct is interaction between elements of human nature and the environment, natural and social.—*Human Nature and Conduct.*

See also: Aims and Purposes 3; Character 2; Children 2; Ideals 2, 5; Society 4; Wisdom 2.

CONSCIENCE

Our intelligence is bound up, so far as its materials are concerned, with the community life of which we are a part. We know what it communicates to us, and know according to the habits it forms in us. . . So with conscience. When a child acts, those about him re-act. They shower encouragement upon him, visit him with approval, or they bestow frowns and rebuke. What others do to us when we act is as natural a consequence of our action as what the fire does to us when we plunge our hands in it. The social environment may be as artificial as you please. But its action in response to ours is natural, not artificial. In language and imagination we rehearse the responses of others just as we dramatically enact other consequences. We foreknow how others will act, and the foreknowledge is the beginning of judgment passed on action. We know with them; there is conscience. An assembly is formed within our breast which discusses and appraises proposed and performed acts. The community without becomes a forum and tribunal within, a judgment-seat of charges, assessments and exculpations. Our thoughts of our own actions are saturated with the ideas that others entertain about them, ideas which have been expressed not only in explicit instruction but still more effectively in reaction to our acts.—*Human Nature and Conduct.*

CONSCIOUSNESS

1. Consciousness is only a very small and shifting portion of experience.—*Essays in Experimental Logic.*

2. To assert that conscious behavior is a fiction is to draw a logical deduction from a premise, not to observe a fact. And since the fact of conscious behavior, of observing, analyzing, noting, reasoning, is involved in the whole undertaking, the absurdity of conclusion shows the falsity of the premise.—*Philosophy and Civilization.*

See also: Aims and Purposes 1; Education 1; Existence; Knowledge 7; Mind 3, 6; Relations 1.

CONSERVATISM

1. Let us admit the case of the conservative: if we once start thinking no one can guarantee what will be the outcome, except that many objects, ends, and institutions will be surely doomed. Every thinker puts some portion of an apparently stable world in peril, and no one can wholly predict what will emerge in its place.—*Characters and Events.*

2. In the world of natural change, men learned control by means of the systematic invention of effective tools only when they gave up preoccupation with lofty principles logically arranged, and occupied themselves seriously with the turmoil of concrete observable changes. Till we accomplish a like revolu-

tion in social and moral affairs, our politics will continue to be an idle spectator of an alternation of social comedies and tragedies, compensating for its impotency by reducing its applause and hisses to a scheme of fixed canons which the show is then imagined to exemplify.—*Ibid.*

3. Men's minds are still pathetically in the clutch of old habits and haunted by old memories.—*Liberalism and Social Action.*

4. The assertion that human nature cannot be changed is heard when social changes are urged as reforms and improvements of existing conditions. It is always heard when the proposed changes in institutions or conditions stand in sharp opposition to what exists. If the conservative were wiser, he would rest his objections in most cases, not upon the unchangeability of human nature, but upon the inertia of custom; upon the resistance that acquired habits offer to change after they are once acquired. It is hard to teach an old dog new tricks and it is harder yet to teach society to adopt customs which are contrary to those which have long prevailed. Conservatism of this type would be intelligent, and it would compel those wanting change not only to moderate their pace, but also to ask how the changes they desire could be introduced with a minimum of shock and dislocation.—*Problems of Men.*

See also: Authority 2.

CREATIVE WORK

1. Every individual is in some way original and creative in his very make-up; that is the meaning of individuality. What is most needed is to get rid of what stifles and chokes its manifestation. When the oppressive and artificial load is removed, each will find his own opportunity for positive constructive work in some field. And it is not the extent, the area, of his work that is important as much as its quality and intensity.— *Construction and Criticism.*

2. Creative activity is our great need; but criticism, self-criticism, is the road to its release.—*Ibid.*

See also: Thinking 12.

CRITICISM

Criticism is discriminating judgment, careful appraisal, and judgment is appropriately termed criticism wherever the subject-matter of discrimination concerns goods or values.—*Experience and Nature.*

See also: Art 7; Creative Work 2; Freedom of Thought 2; Philosophy 8; School 6.

CULTURE

1. Unless culture be a superficial polish, a veneering of mahogany over common wood, it surely is this—the growth of the imagination in flexibility, in scope, and in sympathy.—*The School and Society.*

2. Culture . . . is opposed to the raw and crude. When the "natural" is identified with this rawness, culture is opposed to what is called natural development. Culture is also something personal; it is cultivation with respect to appreciation of ideas and art and broad human interests . . . It is the capacity for constantly expanding the range and accuracy of one's perception of meanings.—*Democracy and Education.*

3. Since we can neither beg nor borrow a culture without betraying both it and ourselves, nothing remains save to produce one.—*Characters and Events.*

4. Each culture has its own individuality and has a pattern that binds its parts together.—*Art as Experience.*

5. The state of culture is a state of interaction of many factors, the chief of which are law and politics, industry and commerce, science and technology, the arts of expression and communication, and of morals, or the values men prize and the

ways in which they evaluate them; and finally, though indirectly, the system of general ideas used by men to justify and to criticize the fundamental conditions under which they live, their social philosophy.—*Freedom and Culture.*

6. The idea of culture . . . points to the conclusion that whatever are the native constituents of human nature, the culture of a period and group is the determining influence in their arrangement; it is that which determines the patterns of behavior that mark out the activities of any group, family, clan, people, sect, faction, class. It is at least as true that the state of culture determines the order and arrangement of native tendencies as that human nature produces any particular set or system of social phenomena so as to obtain satisfaction for itself. The problem is to find out the way in which the elements of a culture interact with each other and the way in which the elements of human nature are caused to interact with one another under conditions set by their interaction with the existing environment. For example, if our American culture is largely a pecuniary culture, it is not because the original or innate structure of human nature tends of itself to obtaining pecuniary profit. It is rather that a certain complex culture stimulates, promotes and consolidates native tendencies so as to produce a certain pattern of desires and purposes.—*Ibid.*

7. No matter what is the native make-up of human nature, its working activities, those which respond to institutions and rules and which finally shape the pattern of the latter, are created by the whole body of occupations, interests, skills, beliefs that constitute a given culture. As the latter changes, especially as it grows complex and intricate in the way in which American life has changed since our political organization took shape, new problems take the place of those governing the earlier formation and distribution of political powers.—*Ibid.*

See also: Education 4, 12; Experience 9; History 6; Liberalism 4.

CURIOSITY

There is no single faculty called "curiosity"; every normal organ of sense and of motor activity is on the *qui vive*. It wants a chance to be active, and it needs some object in order to act. The sum total of these outgoing tendencies constitutes curiosity. It is the basic factor in enlargement of experience.—*How We Think.*

See also: Ignorance; Reading.

D

DECEPTION

No one is deceived so readily as a person under strong emotion.—*Human Nature and Conduct.*

See also: Desire 1; Reality 2.

DEFINITION

1. Definition means essentially the growth of a meaning out of vagueness into definiteness.—*How We Think.*

2. A definition is good when it is sagacious, and it is that when it so points the direction in which we can move expeditiously toward having an experience. Physics and chemistry have learned by the inward necessity of their tasks that a definition is that which indicates to us *how* things are made, and in so far enables to predict their occurrence, to test for their presence and, sometimes, to make them ourselves. Theorists and literary critics have lagged far behind. They are still largely in thrall to the ancient metaphysics of essence according to which a definition, if it is "correct," discloses to us some inward reality.—*Art as Experience.*

DEMOCRACY

1. Modern life means democracy, democracy means freeing intelligence for independent effectiveness—the emancipation of

mind as an individual organ to do its own work. We naturally associate democracy, to be sure, with freedom of action, but freedom of action without freed capacity of thought behind it is only chaos.—"Democracy in Education," in the *Elementary School Teacher*, IV (1903).

2. Democracy inevitably carries with it increased respect for the individual as an individual, greater opportunity for freedom, independence, and initiative in conduct and thought, and correspondingly demand for fraternal regard and for self-imposed and voluntarily borne responsibilities.—"Democracy and Education," in the *Cyclopedia of Education* (ed. by P. Monroe).

3. The devotion of democracy to education is a familiar fact. The superficial explanation is that a government resting upon popular suffrage cannot be successful unless those who elect and who obey their governors are educated. Since a democratic society repudiates the principle of external authority, it must find a substitute in voluntary disposition and interest; these can be created only by education. But there is a deeper explanation. A democracy is more than a form of government; it is primarily a mode of associated living, of conjoint communicated experience. The extension in space of the number of individuals who participate in an interest so that each has to refer his own action to that of others, and to consider the action of others to give point and direction to his own, is equivalent to the breaking down of those barriers of class, race, and national territory which kept men from perceiving the full import of their activity. These more numerous and more varied points of contact denote a greater diversity of stimuli to which an individual has to respond; they consequently put a premium on variation in his action. They secure a liberation of powers which remain suppressed as long as the incitations to action are partial, as they must be in a group which in its exclusiveness shuts out many interests.

The widening of the area of shared concerns, and the liberation of a greater diversity of personal capacities which characterize a democracy, are not of course the product of deliberation and conscious effort. On the contrary, they are caused by the development of modes of manufacture and commerce, travel, migration, and intercommunication which flowed from the command of science over natural energy. But after greater individualization on one hand, and a broader community of interest on the other have come into existence, it is a matter of deliberate effort to sustain and extend them. Obviously a society to which stratification into separate classes would be fatal, must see to it that intellectual opportunities are accessible to all on equable and easy terms. A society marked off into classes need be specially attentive only to the education of its ruling elements. A society which is mobile, which is full of channels for the distribution of a change occurring anywhere, must see to it that its members are educated to personal initiative and adaptability.—*Democracy and Education.*

4. Democracy has many meanings, but if it has a moral meaning, it is found in resolving that the supreme task of all political institutions and industrial governments shall be the contribution they make to the all-round growth of every member of society.—*Reconstruction in Philosophy.*

5. Democracy must begin at home, and its home is the neighborly community.—*The Public and Its Problems.*

6. We have talked a great deal about democracy, and now for the first time we have to make an effort to find out what it is.—*Characters and Events.*

7. The democratic faith is individual in that it asserts the claims of every individual to the opportunity for realization of potentialities unhampered by birth, family status, unequal legal restrictions, and external authority. By the same token it has been social in character. It has recognized that this end for individuals cannot be attained save through a particular type of political and legal institution. Historically, conditions empha-

sized at first the negative phase of this principle: the overthrow of institutions that were autocratic. It is now seen that the positive side of the principle needs attention; namely, the extension of democracy to the creation of the kind of institutions that will effectively and constructively serve the development of all individuals.—In *The Educational Frontier* (with J. L. Childs; a Symposium, ed. by W. L. Kilpatrick).

8. Democracy is much broader than a special political form, a method of conducting government, of making laws and carrying on governmental administration by means of popular suffrage and elected officers. It is that, of course. But it is something broader and deeper than that. The political and governmental phase of democracy is a means, the best means so far found, for realizing ends in the wide domain of human relationships and the development of human personality. It is, as we often say, though without appreciating all that is involved in the saying, a way of life, social and individual. The key-note of democracy as a way of life may be expressed, it seems to me, as the necessity for the participation of every mature human being in formation of the values that regulate the living of men together; which is necessary from the standpoint of both the general social welfare and the full development of human beings as individuals.—"Democracy and Educational Administration," in *School and Society*, XLV (1937).

9. Democratic ends demand democratic methods for their realization.—*Freedom and Culture.*

10. For a long period we acted as if our democracy were something that perpetuated itself automatically; as if our ancestors had succeeded in setting up a machine that solved the problem of perpetual motion in politics. We acted as if democracy were something that took place mainly at Washington and Albany—or some other state capital—under the impetus of what happened when men and women went to the polls once a year or so—which is a somewhat extreme way of saying that

we have had the habit of thinking of democracy as a kind of political mechanism that will work as long as citizens were reasonably faithful in performing political duties.

Of late years we have heard more and more frequently that this is not enough. . . . Democracy as a personal, an individual, way of life involves nothing fundamentally new. But when applied it puts a new practical meaning in old ideas. Put into effect it signifies that powerful present enemies of democracy can be successfully met only by the creation of personal attitudes in individual human beings; that we must get over our tendency to think that its defense can be found in any external means whatever, whether military or civil, if they are separated from individual attitudes so deep-seated as to constitute personal character.

Democracy is a way of life controlled by a working faith in the possibilities of human nature. Belief in the Common Man is a familiar article in the democratic creed. That belief is without basis and significance save as it means faith in the potentialities of human nature as that nature is exhibited in every human being irrespective of race, color, sex, birth, and family, of material or cultural wealth. This faith may be enacted in statutes, but it is only on paper unless it is put in force in the attitudes which human beings display to one another in all the incidents and relations of daily life. To denounce Nazism for intolerance, cruelty and stimulation of hatred amounts to fostering insincerity if, in our personal relations to other persons, if, in our daily walk and conversation, we are moved by racial, color, or other class prejudice; indeed, by anything save a generous belief in their possibilities as human beings, a belief which brings with it the need for providing conditions which will enable these capacities to reach fulfillment. The democratic faith in human equality is belief that every human being, independent of the quantity or range of his personal endowment, has the right to equal opportunity with every other person for development of whatever gifts he has. The democratic belief in the principle of leadership is a generous one. It is universal. It is belief in the capacity of every person to lead his own life free from coercion and imposition by others provided right conditions are supplied.—"Creative Democracy," in *The Philosopher of the Common Man:* Essays in Honor of John Dewey (a Symposium, ed. by W. H. Kilpatrick).

11. Democracy is not an easy road to take and follow. On the contrary, it is as far as its realization is concerned in the complex conditions of the contemporary world a supremely difficult one. Upon the whole we are entitled to take courage from the fact that it has worked as well as it has done. But to this courage we must add, if our courage is to be intelligent rather than blind, the fact that successful maintenance of democracy demands the utmost in the use of the best available methods to procure a social knowledge that is reasonably commensurate with our physical knowledge, and the invention and use of forms of social engineering reasonably commensurate with our technological abilities in physical affairs.—"Democratic Faith and Education," in the *Antioch Review,* IV (1944).

12. The foundation of democracy is faith in the capacities of human nature; faith in human intelligence and in the power of pooled and cooperative experience.—*Problems of Men.*

See also: Differences; Equality; Freedom 9; Intelligence 3; Liberalism 3; School 2, 8, 9; Teaching 6.

DESIRE

1. It is customary to describe desires in terms of their objects, meaning by objects the things which figure as in imagination their goals. As the object is noble or base, so, it is thought, is desire. In any case, emotions rise and cluster about the object.

This stands out so conspicuously in immediate experience that it monopolizes the central position in the traditional psychological theory of desire. Barring gross self-deception or the frustration of external circumstances, the outcome, or end-result, of desire is regarded by this theory as similar to the end-in-view or object consciously desired. Such, however, is not the case, as readily appears from the analysis of deliberation . . .

The object desired and the attainment of desire are no more alike than a signboard on the road is like the garage to which it points and which it recommends to the traveler. Desire is the forward urge of living creatures. When the push and drive of life meets no obstacle, there is nothing which we call desire. There is just life-activity. But obstructions present themselves, and activity is dispersed and divided. Desire is the outcome. It is activity surging forward to break through what dams it up.— *Human Nature and Conduct.*

2. Desire has a powerful influence upon intellectual beliefs. —*A Common Faith.*

3. Need and desire—out of which grow purpose and direction of energy—go beyond what exists. . . . They continually open the way into the unexplored and unattained future.—"Creative Democracy," in *The Philosopher of the Common Man:* Essays in Honor of John Dewey (a Symposium, ed. by W. H. Kilpatrick).

See also: Change 1; Good and Evil 3; Growth 2; Habit 5; Intelligence 2; Open-mindedness 2; Truth 1; Value 5.

DIFFERENCES

To cooperate by giving differences a chance to show themselves because of the belief that the expression of difference is not only a right of the other persons but is a means of enriching one's own life-experience, is inherent in the democratic personal way of life.—"Creative Democracy," in *The Philosopher of the Common Man:* Essays in Honor of John Dewey (a Symposium, ed. by W. H. Kilpatrick).

See also: Pluralism.

DISCIPLINE

1. The discipline of the school should proceed from the life of the school as a whole and not directly from the teacher.— *My Pedagogic Creed.*

2. Discipline means power at command; mastery of the resources available for carrying through the action undertaken. To know what one is to do and to move to do it promptly and by use of the requisite means is to be disciplined, whether we are thinking of an army or a mind. Discipline is positive. To cow the spirit, to subdue inclination, to compel obedience, to mortify the flesh, to make a subordinate perform an uncongenial task—these things are or are not disciplinary according as they do or do not tend to the development of power to recognize what one is about and to persistence in accomplishment.— *Democracy and Education.*

See also: Doubt 1; Education 15; Mind 4; School 2.

DISCUSSION

1. Discussion is communication, and it is by communication that ideas are shared and become a common possession.—Reply in *The Philosophy of John Dewey* (a Symposium, ed. by P. A. Schilpp).

2. Discussion is moral in the degree in which it consists of complaints about what exists and exhortations about what should or ought to exist.—"Liberating the Social Scientist," in the *Commentary,* IV (1947).

See also: School 6; Tolerance 2.

DOUBT

1. The natural man is impatient with doubt and suspense: he impatiently hurries to be shut of it. A disciplined mind takes delight in the problematic, and cherishes it until a way out is found that approves itself upon examination.—*The Quest for Certainty.*

2. We only inquire and form hypotheses which future inquiry will confirm or reject. But such doubts are an incident of faith in the method of intelligence. They are signs of faith, not of a pale and impotent skepticism. We doubt in order that we may find out.—*A Common Faith.*

3. Personal states of doubt that are not evoked by, and are not relative to, some existential situation are pathological; when they are extreme they constitute the mania of doubting.—*Logic: The Theory of Inquiry.*

See also: Inquiry 1; Mind 5; Thinking 5.

DREAMS

1. Dreams are not something outside of the regular course of events; they are in and of it. They are not cognitive distortions of real things; they are *more* real things. There is nothing abnormal in their existence, any more than there is in the bursting of a bottle. But they may be abnormal, from the standpoint of their influence, if their operation as stimuli is calling out responses to modify the future. Dreams have often been taken as prognostics of what is to happen; they have modified conduct.—In the *Creative Intelligence:* Essays in the Pragmatic Attitude (a Symposium).

2. Since I begin with experience as the manifestation of interactions of organism and environment, it follows that the distinction between the things of a dream and of waking life is one to be itself stated in terms of different modes of interac-

tion.—Reply in the *Philosophy of John Dewey* (a Symposium, ed. by P. A. Schilpp).

See also: Nature 2; Reality 2.

DUTY

There is no doubt that the ability to perform an irksome duty is a very useful accomplishment, but the usefulness does not lie in the irksomeness of the task. Things are not useful or necessary because they are unpleasant or tiresome, but in spite of these characteristics.—*Schools of To-Morrow* (with Evelyn Dewey).

See also: Freedom of Thought 2; Teaching 2; Tolerance 2.

E

ECONOMICS

Economics is the science of phenomena due to one love and one aversion—gain and labor.—*Human Nature and Conduct.* *See also*: Labor; Peace; Power 2; Production and Consumption 2.

EDUCATION

1. All education proceeds by the participation of the individual in the social consciousness of the race. This process begins unconsciously almost at birth, and is continually shaping the individual's powers, saturating his consciousness, forming his habits, training his ideas, and arousing his feelings and emotions. Through this unconscious education the individual gradually comes to share in the intellectual and moral resources which humanity has succeeded in getting together. He becomes an inheritor of the funded capital of civilization. The most formal and technical education in the world cannot safely depart from this general process. It can only organize it or differentiate it in some particular direction.—*My Pedagogic Creed.*

2. Education . . . is a process of living and not a preparation for future living.—*Ibid.*

3. Education is the fundamental method of social progress and reform.—*Ibid.;* also *Education Today.*

4. While our educational leaders are talking of culture, the development of personality, etc., as the end and aim of education, the great majority of those who pass under the tuition of the school regard it only as a narrowly practical tool with which to get bread and butter enough to eke out a restricted life.—*The School and Society.*

5. Speaking generally, education signifies the sum total of processes by which a community or social group, whether small or large, transmits its acquired power and aims with a view to securing its own continued existence and growth.—"Education," in the *Cyclopedia of Education* (ed. by P. Monroe).

6. Education may be defined as a process of continuous reconstruction of experience with the purpose of widening and deepening its social content, while, at the same time, the individual gains control of the methods involved.—*Ibid.*

7. The function of education is to help the growing of a helpless young animal into a happy, moral, and efficient human being.—*Schools of To-Morrow* (with Evelyn Dewey).

8. Education is not something to be forced upon children and youth from without, but is the growth of capacities with which human beings are endowed at birth.—*Ibid.*

9. Education which treats all children as if their impulses were those of the average of an adult society is sure to go on reproducing that same average society without even finding out whether and how it might be better.—*Ibid.*

10. The educative process is a continuous process of growth, having as its aim at every stage an added capacity of growth.—*Democracy and Education.*

11. Even in a savage tribe, the achievements of adults are far beyond what the immature members would be capable of if left to themselves. With the growth of civilization, the gap between the original capacities of the immature and the stand-

ards and customs of the elders increases. Mere physical growing up, mere mastery of the bare necessities of subsistence will not suffice to reproduce the life of the group. Deliberate effort and the taking of thoughtful pains are required. Beings who are born not only unaware of, but quite indifferent to, the aims and habits of the social group have to be rendered cognizant of them and actively interested. Education, and education alone, spans the gap.—*Ibid.*

12. The best thing that can be said about any special process of education, like that of the formal school period, is that it renders its subject capable of further education: more sensitive to conditions of growth and more able to take advantage of them. Acquisition of skill, possession of knowledge, attainment of culture are not ends: they are marks of growth and means to its continuing.—*Reconstruction in Philosophy*.

13. Those who received education are those who give it; habits already engendered deeply influence its course. . . . There is no possibility of complete escape from this circle.— "Body and Mind," in the *Bulletin of the N. Y. Academy of Medicine*, IV (1928).

14. We educate for the *status quo* and when the students go forth they do not find anything so settled that it can be called anything of a static kind.—*Education and the Social Order*.

15. The history of educational theory is marked by opposition between the idea that education is development from within and that it is a formation from without; that it is based upon natural endowments and that education is a process of overcoming natural inclinations and substituting in its place habits acquired under external pressure. . . . To imposition from above is opposed expression and cultivation of individuality; to external discipline is opposed free activity; to acquisition of isolated skills and techniques by drill is opposed acquisition of them as means of attaining ends which make direct vital appeal; to preparation for a more or less remote

future is opposed making the most of opportunities of present life; to static aims and materials is opposed acquaintance with a changing world.—*Experience and Education.*

See also: Aims and Purposes 1; Democracy 3; Growth 2, 3; Learning 1; Money 3; School 1, 2, 4, 6, 8, 9; Science 5; Teaching 3.

ENVIRONMENT

1. A being whose activities are associated with others has a social environment. What he does and what he can do depend upon the expectations, demands, approvals, and condemnations of others. A being connected with other beings cannot perform his own activities without taking the activities of others into account. For they are the indispensable conditions of the realization of his tendencies. When he moves he stirs them and reciprocally. We might as well try to imagine a business man doing business, buying and selling, all by himself, as to conceive it possible to define the activities of an individual in terms of his isolated actions.—*Democracy and Education.*

2. Complete adaptation to environment means death. The essential point in all response is the desire to control the environment.—From a *Lecture,* September 29, 1924.

3. Whatever else organic life is or is not, it is a process of activity that involves an environment. It is a transaction extending beyond the spatial limits of the organism. An organism does not live *in* an environment; it lives by means of an environment. Breathing, the ingestion of food, the ejection of waste products, are cases of direct integration; the circulation of the blood and the energizing of the nervous system are relatively indirect. But every organic function is an interaction of intra-organic and extra-organic energies, either directly or indirectly. For life involves expenditure of energy and the energy expended can be replenished only as the activities performed

succeed in making return drafts upon the environment—the only source of restoration of energy. Not even a hibernating animal can live indefinitely upon itself. The energy that is drawn is not forced in from without; it is a consequence of energy expended. If there is a surplus balance, growth occurs. If there is a deficit balance, degeneration commences.

It follows that with every differentiation of structure the environment expands. For a new organ provides a new way of interacting in which things in the world that were previously indifferent enter into life-functions. The environment of an animal that is locomotor differs from that of a sessile plant; that of a jellyfish differs from that of a trout, and the environment of any fish differs from that of a bird. So, to repeat what was just said, the difference is not just that a fish lives in the water and a bird in the air, but that the characteristic functions of these animals are what they are because of the special way in which water and air enter into their respective activities.— *Logic: the Theory of Inquiry.*

4. The fine old saying "A sound mind in a sound body" can and should be extended to read "A sound human being in a sound human environment." The mere change in wording is nothing. A change in aims and methods of working in that direction would mean more than any of us can estimate. Is there anything in the whole business of politics, economics, morals, education—indeed in any profession—save the construction of a proper human environment that will serve, by its very existence, to produce sound and whole human beings, who in turn will maintain a sound and healthy human environment? This is the universal and all-embracing human task.—In *Intelligence in the Modern World* (ed. by J. Ratner).

5. If we could look into the minds of our neighbors, I think we should not be much surprised to find in them quite frequently the notion that a man exists within the boundaries which are visible, tangible, and observable. In a word, the

man is identified with what is underneath his skin. We incline to suppose that we would know all about him if we could find out everything that is happening in his brain and other parts of his nervous system: in his glands, muscles, viscera, heart and lungs, and so on. Now up to a certain point we are on the right track, provided we emphasize sufficiently the interaction, the working together, of all these diverse processes. We can get a better idea of the unity of the human being as we know more about all these processes and the way they work together, as they check and stimulate one another and bring about a balance. But the one positive point I wish to present is that while this is necessary it is not enough. We must observe and understand these internal processes and their interactions from the standpoint of their interaction with what is going on outside the skin—with that which is called the environment—if we are to obtain a genuine conception of the unity of the human being.

Our attitude with respect to this matter is a strange mixture. In special points we take for granted the inclusion of the conditions and energies that are outside the boundaries set by the skin. No one supposes for a moment that there can be respiration without the surrounding air; or that the lungs are anything more than organs of interaction with what is outside the body. No one thinks of separating the processes of digestion from connection with foodstuffs derived by means of other organs from the environment. We know that eye, ear and hand, and somatic musculature, are concerned with objects and events outside the boundaries of the body. These things we take for granted so regularly and unconsciously that it seems foolish to mention them. . . . The strangeness of the mixture of which I spoke consists in the fact that while we recognize the involvement of conditions external to the body in all organic processes, when they are taken one by one, we often fail to recognize and act upon the idea as an inclusive principle by which to understand the unity of man.—*Ibid.*

See also: Experience 3, 7; Human Nature 1; Individuality 2; Life 2; Morality 1, 8; Moral Science; Teaching 3; Thinking 14; World 3; Youth 1.

EQUALITY

Belief in equality is an element of the democratic credo. It is not, however, belief in equality of natural endowments. Those who proclaimed the idea of equality did not suppose they were enunciating a psychological doctrine, but a legal and political one. All individuals are entitled to equality of treatment by law and its administration. Each one is affected equally in quality if not in quantity by the institutions under which he lives and has an equal right to express his judgment, although the weight of his judgment may not be equal in amount when it enters into the pooled result to that of others. In short, each one is equally an individual and entitled to equal opportunity of development of his own capacities, be they large or small in range. Moreover, each has needs of his own, as significant to him as those of others are to them. The very fact of natural and psychological inequality is all the more reason for establishment by law of equality of opportunity, since otherwise the former becomes a means of oppression of the less gifted.—*Problems of Men.*

See also: Democracy 10.

EVOLUTION

Man may be one form through which the course of evolution passes; but that is all that he can be. What then . . . is the sense of talking about the goal of the process of evolution being a goal for man, except that it be something in which he is absorbed, swallowed up, forever lost?—"Ethics and Physical Science," in *Andover Review*, VII (1887).

See also: Self 4.

EXISTENCE

Existence means existence for consciousness.—"The Psychological Standpoint," in the *Mind,* XI (1886).

See also: Cause and Effect 1; Discussion 2; Good and Evil 2; Reality 4.

EXPERIENCE

1. The nature of experience can be understood only by noting that it includes an active and a passive element peculiarly combined. On the active hand, experience is *trying*—a meaning which is made explicit in the connected term experiment. On the passive, it is *undergoing*. When we experience something we act upon it, we do something with it; then we suffer or undergo the consequences. We do something to the thing and then it does something to us in return: such is the peculiar combination. The connection of these two phases of experience measures the fruitfulness or value of the experience. Mere activity does not constitute experience. It is dispersive, centrifugal, dissipating. Experience as trying involves change, but change is meaningless transition unless it is consciously connected with the return wave of consequences which flow from it. When an activity is continued *into* the undergoing of consequences, when the change made by action is reflected back into a change made in us, the mere flux is loaded with significance. We learn something. . . .

Blind and capricious impulses hurry us on heedlessly from one thing to another. So far as this happens, everything is writ in water. There is none of that cumulative growth which makes an experience in any vital sense of that term. On the other hand, many things happen to us in the way of pleasure and pain which we do not connect with any prior activity of our own. There is no before or after to such experience; no retrospect nor outlook, and consequently no meaning. We get nothing which may be carried over to foresee what is likely to happen next, and no gain in ability to adjust ourselves to what is coming—no added control. Only by courtesy can such an experience be called experience. To "learn from experience" is to make a backward and forward connection between what we do to things and what we enjoy or suffer from things in consequence. Under such conditions, doing becomes a trying; an experiment with the world to find out what it is like; the undergoing becomes instruction—discovery of the connection of things.—*Democracy and Education.*

2. Where there is experience, there is a living being.—In the *Creative Intelligence:* Essays in the Pragmatic Attitude (a Symposium).

3. In the orthodox view, experience is regarded primarily as a knowledge-affair. But to eyes not looking through ancient spectacles, it assuredly appears as an affair of the intercourse of a living being with its psychical and social environment.—*Ibid.*

4. Experience is *of* as well as *in* nature. It is not experience which is experienced, but nature—stones, plants, animals, diseases, health, temperature, electricity, and so on. Things interacting in certain ways are experience; they are what is experienced. Linked in certain other ways with another natural object—the human organism—they are *how* things are experienced as well.—*Experience and Nature.*

5. Experience cannot deliver to us necessary truths; truths completely demonstrated by reason. Its conclusions are particular, not universal.—*The Quest for Certainty.*

6. Experience in the degree in which it is experience is heightened vitality.—*Art as Experience.*

7. Experience is a matter of the interaction of organism with its environment, an environment that is human as well as physical, that includes the materials of tradition and institutions as well as local surroundings. . . . Because every experience is

constituted by interaction between "subject" and "object," between a self and its world, it is not itself either merely physical nor merely mental, no matter how much one factor or the other predominates.—*Ibid.*

8. All direct experience is qualitative, and qualities are what make life experience itself directly precious.—*Ibid.*

9. I have held that experience is a matter or an "affair" of interaction of living creatures with their environment; human experience being what it is because human beings are subject to the influence of culture, including use of definite means of intercommunication, and are what in anthropological jargon are called acculturated organisms. Reply in the *Philosophy of John Dewey* (a Symposium, ed. by P. A. Schilpp).

See also: Abstraction 1; Art 3, 5; Communication; Consciousness 1; Curiosity; Education 5; Inference 4; Knowledge 1; Language 2, 4; Man 1; Memory; Objects 2; School 8; Self 6; Society 2, 3.

EXPERIMENTAL METHOD

1. The experimental method . . . means that we have no right to call anything knowledge except where our activity actually produced certain physical changes in things, which agree with and confirm the conception entertained. Short of such specific changes, our beliefs are only hypotheses, theories, suggestions, guesses, and are to be entertained tentatively and to be utilized as indications of experiments to be tried.—*Democracy and Education.*

2. Experimental method is something other than the use of blow-pipes, retorts and reagents. It is the foe of every belief that permits habit and wont to dominate invention and discovery, and ready-made system to override verifiable fact. Constant revision is the work of experimental inquiry.—*Individualism, Old and New.*

3. Experimental method is fatal to dogmatism because it shows that all ideas, conceptions, theories, however extensive and self-consistent and esthetically attractive they may be, are to be entertained provisionally until they have been tested by acting upon them. To state the fact in its full force, ideas prior to active test are intellectually significant only as guides and as plans of possible actions. The actions when undertaken produce consequences which test, expand, and modify the ideas previously tentatively entertained. The experimental method is thus opposed once and for all to all methods which claim to be sure-fire.—In *The Educational Frontier* (a Symposium, ed. by W. H. Kilpatrick).

4. Experimental method is not just messing around nor doing a little of this and a little of that in the hope that things will improve. Just as in the physical sciences, it implies a coherent body of ideas, a theory, that gives direction to effort.—*Problems of Men.*

See also: Liberalism 4; Scientific Method.

F

FACTS

1. Social facts are themselves natural facts.—"Social as a Category," in *The Monist*, XXXVIII (1928).

2. The ideal of the knowledge dealing with physical facts is the elimination of all factors dependent upon distinctively human response. "First," physically speaking, is the ultimate residue after human purposes, desires, emotions, ideas and ideals have been systematically excluded. A social "fact," on the other hand, is a concretion in external form of precisely these human factors. An occurrence is a physical fact only when its constituents and their relations remain the same, irrespective of the human attitude toward them. A species of mosquitoes is the carrier of the germs of malaria, whether we like or dislike malaria. Drainage and oil-spraying to destroy mosquitoes are a social fact because their use depends upon purpose and desire. A steam locomotive or a dynamo is a physical fact in its structure; it is a social fact when its existence depends upon the desire for rapid and cheap transportation and communication. The machine itself may be understood physically without reference to human aim and motive. But the railway or public-utility system cannot be under-

stood without reference to human purposes and human consequences.—"Social Science and Social Control," in *The New Republic*, LXVII (1931).

See also: Experimental Method 2; Hypotheses 3; Inference 2; Openmindedness 2; Science 4; Theory 4.

FAITH

1. Ours is the responsibility of conserving, transmitting, rectifying and expanding the heritage of values we have received that those who come after us may receive it more solid and secure, more widely accessible and more generously shared than we have received it. Here are all the elements for a religious faith that shall not be confined to sect, class or race. Such a faith has always been implicitly the common faith of mankind. It remains to make it explicit and militant.—*A Common Faith*.

2. Were we to admit that there is but one method for ascertaining fact and truth—that conveyed by the word "scientific" in its most general and generous sense—no discovery in any branch of knowledge and inquiry could then disturb the faith that is religious. I should describe this faith as the unification of the self through allegiance to inclusive ideal ends, which imagination presents to us and to which the human will responds as worthy of controlling our desires and choices.—*Ibid*.

See also: Democracy 12; Doubt 2; Religion 9.

FATE

Man is capable, if he will but exercise the required courage, intelligence and effort, of shaping his own fate. Physical conditions offer no unsurmountable barriers.—*Reconstruction in Philosophy*.

FORCE

Dependence on force sooner or later calls out force on the other side.—*Problems of Men.*

See also: Value 1; War 2.

FREEDOM

1. Freedom is the "release of capacity from whatever hems it in."—*Reconstruction in Philosophy.*

2. We are free in the degree in which we act knowing what we are about. The identification of freedom with "freedom of the will" locates contingency in the wrong place.—*The Quest for Certainty.*

3. We are free not because of what we statically are, but in so far as we are becoming different from what we have been.—*Philosophy and Civilization.*

4. Freedom is not something that can be handed to men as a gift from outside, whether by old-fashioned dynastic benevolent despotism or by new-fashioned dictatorship, whether of the proletarian or of the fascist order. It is something which can be had only as individuals participate in winning it, and this fact, rather than some particular political mechanism, is the essence of democratic liberalism.—*Liberalism and Social Action.*

5. In ultimate analysis, freedom is important because it is a condition both of realization of the potentialities of an individual and of social progress. Without light, a people perishes. Without freedom, light grows dim and darkness comes to reign. Without freedom, old truths become so stale and worn that they cease to be truths and become mere dictates of external authority. Without freedom, search for new truths and the disclosure of new paths in which humanity may walk more assuredly and justly come to an end. Freedom which is liberation for the individual, is the ultimate assurance of the

movement of society toward more humane and noble ends. He who would put the freedom of others in bond, especially freedom of inquiry and communication, creates conditions which finally imperil his own freedom and that of his off-spring. Eternal vigilance is the price of the conservation and extension of freedom, and the schools should be the ceaseless guardians and creators of this vigilance.—"Academic Freedom," in *Intelligence in the Modern World* (ed. by J. Ratner).

6. What is freedom and why is it prized? Is desire for freedom inherent in human nature or is it a product of special circumstances? Is it wanted as an end or as a means of getting other things? Does its possession entail responsibilities, and are these responsibilities so onerous that the mass of men will readily surrender liberty for the sake of greater ease? Is the struggle for liberty so arduous that most men are easily distracted from the endeavor to achieve and maintain it? Does freedom in itself and in the things it brings with it seem as important as security of livelihood; as food, shelter, clothing, or even as having a good time? Did man ever care as much for it as we in this country have been taught to believe? Is there any truth in the old notion that the driving force in political history has been the effort of the common man to achieve freedom? Was our own struggle for political independence in any genuine sense animated by desire for freedom, or were there a number of discomforts that our ancestors wanted to get rid of, things having nothing in common save that they were felt to be troublesome?—*Freedom and Culture.*

7. Men may be brought by long habit to hug their chains.—*Ibid.*

8. If we want individuals to be free we must see to it that suitable conditions exist.—*Ibid.*

9. Everything that bars freedom and fullness of communication sets up barriers that divide human beings into sets and cliques, into antagonistic sects and factions, and thereby

undermines the democratic way of life.—"Creative Democracy," in *The Philosopher of the Common Man*: Essays in Honor of John Dewey (a Symposium, ed. by W. H. Kilpatrick).

10. The democratic idea of freedom is not the right of each individual to do as he pleases, even if it be qualified by adding "provided he does not interfere with the same freedom on the part of others." While the idea is not always, not often enough, expressed in words, the basic freedom is that of freedom of mind and of whatever degree of freedom of action and experience is necessary to produce freedom of intelligence. The modes of freedom guaranteed by the Bill of Rights are of this nature: Freedom of belief and conscience, of expression of opinion, of assembly for discussion and conference, of the press as an organ of communication. They are guaranteed because without them individuals are not free to develop and society is deprived of what they might contribute.—*Problems of Men*.

See also: Authority 1, 2; Democracy 1, 7.

FREEDOM OF THOUGHT

1. It has often been assumed that freedom of speech, oral or written, is independent of freedom of thought, and that you cannot take the latter away in any case, since it goes on inside of minds where it cannot be got at. No idea could be more mistaken. . . . If ideas when aroused cannot be communicated, they either fade away or become warped and morbid. —*Philosophy and Civilization*.

2. We may felicitate ourselves that we live where free discussion and free criticism are still values which are not denied us by some power reaching out for a monopoly of cultural and spiritual life. The inability of human beings in so many parts of the world to engage in free exchange of ideas should make

us aware, by force of contrast, of the privilege we still enjoy and of our duty of defending and extending it. It should make us aware that free thought itself, free inquiry, is crippled and finally paralyzed by suppression of free communication.

Such communication includes the right and responsibility of submitting every idea and every belief to severest criticism. It is less important that we all believe alike than that we all alike inquire freely and put at the disposal of one another such glimpses as we may obtain of the truth for which we are in search.—Reply in *The Philosophy of John Dewey* (a Symposium, ed. by P. A. Schilpp).

See also: Democracy 1; Freedom 10.

FRIENDSHIP

In friendship . . . the interests and modes of response of another become an expansion of our own being. We learn to see with his eyes, hear with his ears.—*Art as Experience*.

FUTURE

1. The Golden Age lies ahead of us, not behind us.—*Reconstruction in Philosophy*.

2. The present activity is the only one really under control. . . . Control of future living, such as it may turn out to be, is wholly dependent upon taking his present activity, seriously and devotedly, as an end, not as a means. And a man has his hands full in doing well what now needs to be done.—*Human Nature and Conduct*.

3. The future that is foreseen is a future that is sometime to be present.—*Ibid*.

4. To the being fully alive, the future is not ominous but a promise; it surrounds the present as a halo. It consists of pos-

sibilities that are felt as a possession of what is now and here.—*Art as Experience.*

See also: Change; Desire 3; Education 2, 15; Growth 3; Philosophers 4; Science 2.

G

GOD

The word "God," on one score, can mean only a particular being. On the other score, it denotes the unity of all ideal ends arousing us to desire and actions. Does this unification have a claim upon our attitude and conduct because it is already, apart from us, in realized existence, or because of its own inherent meaning and value? Suppose for the moment that the word "God" means the ideal ends that at a given time and place one acknowledges as having authority over his volition and emotion, the values to which one is supremely devoted, as far as these ends, through imagination, take on unity. If we make this supposition, the issue will stand out clearly in contrast with the doctrine of religions that "God" designates some kind of Being having prior and therefore non-ideal existence.—*A Common Faith.*

GOOD AND EVIL

1. Non-resistance to evil which takes the form of paying no attention to it is a way of promoting it.—*Human Nature and Conduct.*

2. When we have used our thought to its utmost and have thrown into the moving unbalanced balance of things our puny

strength, we know that though the universe slay us we may trust, for our lot is one with whatever is good in existence. We know that such thought and effort is one condition of the coming into existence of the better.—*The Philosophy of John Dewey* (ed. by J. Ratner).

3. In its relation to desire . . . the good is that which satisfies want, craving, which fulfills or makes complete the need which stirs to action. In its relation to thought, or as an idea of an object to be attained, it imposes upon those about to act the necessity for rational insight, or moral wisdom. For experience shows that not every satisfaction of appetite and craving turns out to be a good; many ends *seem* good while we are under the influence of strong passion, which in actual experience and in such thought as might have occurred in a cool moment are actually bad. The task of moral theory is thus to frame a theory of Good as the end or objective of desire, and also to frame a theory of the true, as distinct from the specious, good. —*Ethics* (with J. H. Tufts; revised ed.).

See also: Ideals 3; Progress 3; Right 1, 2.

GOVERNMENT

No government by experts in which the masses do not have the chance to inform the experts as to their needs can be anything but an oligarchy managed in the interests of the few. —*The Public and Its Problems*.

See also: Democracy 3, 4, 8.

GROWTH

1. The dominant vocation of all human beings at all times is living—intellectual and moral growth.—*Democracy and Education*.

2. Since growth is the characteristic of life, education is all one with growing; it has no end beyond itself. The criterion of

the value of school education is the extent in which it creates a desire for continued growth and supplies means for making the desire effective in fact.—*Ibid.*

3. If education is growth, it must progressively realize present possibilities, and thus make individuals better fitted to cope with later requirements. Growing is not something which is complete in odd moments; it is a continuous leading into the future. If the environment, in school and out, supplies conditions which utilize adequately the present capacities of the immature, the future which grows out of the present is surely taken care of.—*Ibid.*

See also: Definition 1; Democracy 4; Education 10, 11, 12; Environment 3; Experience 1; Interest 2.

H

HABIT

1. Routine habits are unthinking habits; "bad" habits are habits so severed from reason that they are opposed to the conclusions of conscious deliberation and decision. As we have seen, the acquiring of habits is due to an original plasticity of our natures: to our ability to vary responses till we find an appropriate and efficient way of acting. Routine habits, and habits that possess us instead of our possessing them, are habits which put an end to plasticity. They mark the close of power to vary.—*Democracy and Education.*

2. Men cannot easily throw off their old habits of thinking, and never can throw off all of them at once.—*Reconstruction in Philosophy.*

3. Habits are conditions of intellectual efficiency. They operate in two ways upon intellect. Obviously, they restrict its reach, they fix its boundaries. They are blinders that confine the eyes of mind to the road ahead. They prevent thought from straying away from its imminent occupation to a landscape more varied and picturesque but irrelevant to practice. Outside the scope of habits, thought works gropingly, fumbling in confused uncertainty; and yet habit made complete in routine shuts in thought so effectually that it is no longer

needed or possible. The routineer's road is a ditch out of which he cannot get, whose sides enclose him, directing his course so thoroughly that he no longer thinks of his path or his destination. All habit-forming involves the beginning of an intellectual specialization which if unchecked ends in thoughtless action.—*Human Nature and Conduct.*

4. Habit is energy organized in certain channels.—*Ibid.*

5. We cannot change habit directly: that notion is magic. But we can change it indirectly by modifying conditions, by an intelligent selecting and weighing of the objects which engage attention and which influence the fulfillment of desires. —*Ibid.*

6. While it is admitted that the word habit has been used in a somewhat broader sense than is usual, we must protest against the tendency in psychological literature to limit its meaning to repetition. . . . Tendency to repeat acts is an incident of many habits but not of all. A man with the habit of giving way to anger may show his habit by a murderous attack upon some one who has offended. His act is nonetheless due to habit because it occurs only once in his life. The essence of habit is an acquired predisposition to ways or modes of response, not to particular acts except as, under special conditions, these express a way of behaving.—*Human Nature and Conduct.*

See also: Character 2; Conscience; Education 13, 15; Experimental Method 2; Knowledge 7; Responsibility 2.

HAPPINESS

1. Because all men want to be happy, it hardly follows that every man wants all to be happy.—*Outlines of a Critical Theory of Ethics.*

2. Suppose we drop the hedonistic emphasis upon states of pleasure and pain and substitute the wider, or vaguer, ideal of

well-being, welfare, happiness, as the proper standard of approval.—*Ethics* (with J. H. Tufts; revised ed.).

See also: Individual 1.

HISTORY

1. It is difficult to avoid reading the past in terms of the contemporary scene.—*Liberalism and Social Action*.

2. All historical construction is necessarily selective.—*Logic: the Theory of Inquiry*.

3. As culture changes, the conceptions that are dominant in a culture change. . . . History is then rewritten.—*Ibid*.

See also: Freedom 6; Liberalism 4; Loyalty 2; Peace; Philosophers 4; Philosophy 4; Symbols 2.

HUMAN CONCERNS

We are not the creators of heaven and earth; we have no responsibility for their operations save as their motions are altered by our movements. Our concern is with the significance of that slight fraction of total activity which starts from ourselves. The best laid plans of men as well as of mice gang aglee, and for the same reason: inability to dominate the future. The power of man and mouse is infinitely constricted in comparison with the power of events.—*Human Nature and Conduct*.

See also: Culture 2.

HUMANITY

We who now live are parts of a humanity that extends itself into the remote past, a humanity that has interacted with nature. The things in civilization we most prize are not of ourselves. They exist by grace of the doings and sufferings of

the continuous human community in which we are a link.
—*A Common Faith.*

See also: Education 1; Freedom 5; Ideals 7.

HUMAN NATURE

1. Circumstances may change, but human nature remains from age to age the same. Heredity is more potent than environment, and human heredity is untouched by human intent. —*Human Nature and Conduct.*

2. Everything which is distinctively human is learned, not native, even though it could not be learned without native structures which mark man off from other animals.—*The Public and Its Problems.*

3. Any notion that human action is identical with that of nonliving things or with that of the "lower" animals is silly. It is contradicted by the fact that behavior is so organized in human beings as to have for its consequence all that we call civilization, culture, law, arts—fine and industrial—language, morals, institutions, science itself. And by its fruits we know it. Organic processes are thus seen to be the constituent means of a behavior which is endued with purpose and meaning, animate with affection, and informed by recollection and foresight.—*Philosophy and Civilization.*

4. Are contemporary political and economic institutions necessary products of human nature? Or, more generally, does the very constitution of human nature show that certain social arrangements are likely to be successful while others are doomed to failure? Is war, for example, inevitable because of facts of human nature? Is self-interest so ingrained in human nature that the attempt to base industry on anything except a competitive struggle for private gain is sure to fail?—"Human Nature," in the *Encyclopedia of the Social Sciences*, VII.

5. The theory that human nature is unchangeable is the

most depressing and pessimistic of all possible doctrines. If it were carried out logically, it would mean a doctrine of pre-destination from birth that would outdo the most rigid of theological doctrines. For according to it, persons are what they are at birth and nothing can be done about it, beyond the kind of training that an acrobat might give to the muscular system with which he is originally endowed. If a person is born with criminal tendencies, a criminal he will become and remain. If a person is born with an excessive amount of greed, he will become a person living by predatory activities at the expense of others; and so on. I do not doubt at all the existence of differences in natural endowment. But what I am question-ing is the notion that they doom individuals to a fixed channel of expression. It is difficult indeed to make a silk purse out of a sow's ear. But the particular form which, say, a natural musical endowment will take depends upon the social in-fluence to which he is subjected.—*Problems of Men.*

6. Human is as human does.—*Ibid.*

See also: Change; Civilization 5; Conservatism 4; Culture 3, 4; Democracy 12; Freedom 6; Law 2; Morality 4; Moral Science; Religion 2; War 1; Work.

HYPOTHESES

1. Hypotheses are fruitful when they are suggested by actual need, are bulwarked by knowledge already attained, and are tested by the consequences of the operations they evoke. . . . Otherwise imagination is dissipated into fantasies and rises vaporously into the clouds.—*The Quest for Certainty.*

2. It is notorious that a hypothesis does not have to be true in order to be highly serviceable in the conduct of inquiry.— *Logic: the Theory of Inquiry.*

3. The primary value of hypotheses and theories is found in their power to direct observation in discovery of newly ob-

served facts and in their power to organize facts in such a way as to forward the solution of a problem. . . . What a scientist asks of his hypotheses is that they be fruitful in giving direction to his observations and reasonings. Confrontation with an observed fact which does not square with an hypothesis is consequently just as welcome as one which does—since it enables him to introduce modifications into his idea that renders the latter more efficient in future conduct of inquiry. Whereas if a liar is confronted with something which contradicts what he says, there is one hundred per cent nullification of what he has said, with no opportunity allowed for additional development because of the negative confrontation that has occurred. In science, discovery of an exception, of a fact that contradicts a theory in the form in which it has been previously held, is a positive means of advance. It is not only welcome when hit upon but is actively searched for.—Reply in *The Philosophy of John Dewey* (a Symposium, ed. by P. A. Schilpp).

See also: Belief 1; Doubt 2; Experimental Method; Ideas 4; Problems.

I

IDEALS

1. Ideals are held up to follow; standards are given to work by; laws are provided to guide action. . . . If they cannot do this, not merely by accident, but of their own intrinsic nature, they are worse than inert.—*Educational Essays* (ed. by J. J. Findlay).

2. If philosophers could aid in making it clear to a troubled humanity that ideals are continuous with natural events, that they but represent their possibilities, and that recognized possibilities form methods for a conduct which may realize them in fact, philosophers would enforce the sense of a social calling and responsibility.—*Essays in Experimental Logic.*

3. Every ideal . . . projects in securer and wider and fuller form some good which has been previously experienced in a precarious, accidental, fleeting way.—*Human Nature and Conduct.*

4. The ideal is itself the product of discontent with conditions.—*Ibid.*

5. Since the ideal ends are so remotely and accidentally connected with immediate and urgent conditions that need attention, after lip service is given to them, men naturally devote themselves to the latter. If a bird in the hand is worth two in

a neighboring bush, an actuality in hand is worth, for the direction of conduct, many ideals that are so remote as to be invisible and inaccessible. Men hoist the banner of the ideal, and then march in the direction that concrete conditions suggest and reward.—*The Quest for Certainty.*

6. Not all who say, *Ideals, Ideals,* shall enter the kingdom of ideal, but only those shall enter who know and who respect the roads that conduct to the kingdom.—*Characters and Events.*

7. Ideals change as they are applied in existent conditions. The process endures and advances with the life of humanity. What one person and one group accomplish becomes the standing ground and starting point of those who succeed them.—*A Common Faith.*

See also: Faith 2; God; Machine 2; Possibility 2; Religion 2, 9; Theory 4; Thinking 12.

IDEAS

1. Ideas are not genuine ideas unless they are tools with which to search for material to solve a problem.—*How We Think.*

2. Take away ideas and what follows from them, and man seems no better than the beasts of the field.—*The Quest for Certainty.*

3. The test of ideas, of thinking generally, is found in the consequences of the acts to which the ideas lead, that is in the new arrangements of things which are brought into existence. —*Ibid.*

4. Ideas are only tentative or working hypotheses until they are modified, rejected or confirmed by the consequences produced by acting upon them.—"Logic," in the *Encyclopedia of the Social Sciences,* IX.

See also: Abstraction 3; Action 2; Discussion 1; Experimental Method 3, 4; Ignorance; Philosophy 5; Society 3; Words 2, 4.

IGNORANCE

Genuine ignorance is . . . profitable because it is likely to be accompanied by humility, curiosity, and open-mindedness; whereas ability to repeat catch-phrases, cant terms, familiar propositions, gives conceit of learning and coats the mind with a varnish waterproof to new ideas.—*How We Think.*

See also: School 6.

INDIVIDUAL

1. Any given individual is naturally an erratic mixture of fierce insistence upon his own welfare and of profound susceptibility to the happiness of others—different individuals varying much in the respective intensities and proportions of the two tendencies.—*Ethics* (with J. H. Tufts).

2. The cause of modern civilization stands and falls with the ability of the individual to serve as its agent and bearer. —*The Influence of Darwin on Philosophy and Other Essays.*

3. Society is individuals-in-their-relations. An individual apart from social relations is a myth—or monstrosity.—In *The Educational Frontier* (with J. L. Childs; a Symposium, ed. by W. H. Kilpatrick).

See also: Authority 2; Democracy 2, 3, 7; Education 1, 6; Interaction 2; Liberalism 2; Liberty 5; Religion 2; Security 2; State 4.

INDIVIDUALITY

1. Individuality is not originally given but is created under the influence of associated life—*Reconstruction in Philosophy.*

2. Individuality in a social and moral sense is something to

be wrought out. It means initiative, inventiveness, varied resourcefulness, assumption of responsibility in choice of belief and conduct. These are not gifts but achievements. As achievements, they are not absolute, but relative to the use that is made of them. And this use varies with the environment.—*Ibid.*

See also: Creative Work 1; Culture 4; Education 15; Liberalism 4; Loyalty 2; Pluralism.

INFERENCE

1. In every case of reflective activity, a person finds himself confronted with a given, present situation from which he has to arrive at, or conclude to, something else that is not present. This process of arriving at an idea of what is absent on the basis of what is at hand is inference. What is present carries or bears the mind over to the idea and ultimately the acceptance of something else. . . Every inference, just because it goes beyond ascertained and known facts, which are given either by observation or by recollection of prior knowledge, involves a jump from the known to the unknown.—*How We Think.*

2. It is the rare mind that can get relations or draw conclusions from simply hearing facts. Most people must see and handle things before they can tell how these things will behave and what their meaning is.—*Schools of To-Morrow* (with Evelyn Dewey).

3. Inference is the advance into the unknown, the use of established to win the new worlds from the void.—*Essays in Experimental Logic.*

4. Experience taken free of the restrictions imposed by the older concept, is full of inference. There is, apparently, no conscious experience without inference; reflection is native and constant.—In the *Creative Intelligence*: Essays in the Pragmatic Attitude (a Symposium).

See also: Thinking 11.

INQUIRY

1. The existence of inquiries is not a matter of doubt. They enter into every area of life and into every aspect of every area. In everyday living men examine; they turn things over intellectually; they infer and judge as "naturally" as they reap and sow, produce and exchange commodities. As a mode of conduct, inquiry is as accessible to objective study as are these other modes of behavior.—*Logic: the Theory of Inquiry.*

2. To see that a situation requires inquiry is the initial step in inquiry.—*Ibid.*

3. Inquiry is the controlled or directed transformation of an indeterminate situation into one that is so determinate in its constituent distinctions and relations as to convert the elements of the original situation into a unified whole.—*Ibid.*

See also: Belief 3; Doubt 2; Pragmatism 2; Science 4, 8; Teaching 5; Truth 4.

INSANITY

One can be insane without knowing he is insane and one may know insanity without being crazy; indeed absence of the direct experience is said to be an indispensable condition of study of insanity.—*Experience and Nature.*

See also: Power 1; Reality 2.

INTELLIGENCE

1. Intelligence becomes ours in the degree in which we use it and accept responsibility for consequences.—*Human Nature and Conduct.*

2. Intelligence converts desire into plans.—*Ibid.*

3. While what we call intelligence be distributed in unequal amounts, it is the democratic faith that it is sufficiently general so that each individual has something to contribute, whose value can be assessed only as it enters into the final pooled in-

telligence constituted by the contributions of all.—*Problems of Men*.

See also: Aims and Purposes 1; Democracy 12; Knowledge 3; Liberal Education; Liberalism 2; Mistakes; Problems 1; Reason 1; School 2; Theory 3; Understanding 2.

INTERACTION AND INTERDEPENDENCE

1. Nothing in the universe, not even physical things, exist apart from some form of association; there is nothing from the atom to man which is not involved in conjoint action. Planets exist and act in solar systems, and these systems are galaxies. Plants and animals exist and act in conditions of much more intimate and complete interaction and interdependence. Human beings are generated only by union of individuals; the human infant is so feeble in his powers as to be dependent upon the care and protection of others; he cannot grow up without the help given by others; his mind is nourished by contact with others and by intercommunication; as soon as the individual graduates from family life he finds himself taken into other associations, neighborhood, school, village, professional or business associates. Apart from the ties which bind him to others, he is nothing. Even the hermit and Robinson Crusoe, as far as they live on a plane higher than that of the brutes, continue even in physical isolation to be what they are, to think the thoughts which go through their minds, to entertain their characteristic aspirations, because of social connections which existed in the past and which still persist in their imagination and emotions.—*Ethics* (with J. H. Tufts; revised ed.).

2. Individuals are interdependent. No one is born except in dependence on others. Without aid and nurture from others, he would miserably perish. The material of his intellectual subsistence, as well as of his physical, comes to him from others. As he matures, he becomes more physically and economically

independent; but he can carry on his calling only through co-operation and competition with others; he has needs which are satisfied only through exchange of services and commodities. His recreations as well as his achievements are dependent upon sharing with others. The idea that individuals are born separate and isolated and are brought into society only through some artificial device is a pure myth. Social ties and connections are as natural and inevitable as are physical. Even when a person is alone he thinks with language that is derived from association with others, and thinks about questions and issues that have been born in intercourse. Independence of character and judgment is to be prized. But it is an independence which does not signify separateness; it is something displayed in relation to others. There is no one, for example, of whom independent inquiry, reflection, and insight are more characteristic than the genuine scientific and philosophic thinker. But his independence is a futile eccentricity unless he thinks upon problems which have originated in a long tradition, and unless he intends to share his conclusions with others, so as to win their assent or elicit their corrections. Such facts are familiar and commonplace. Their meaning is not always so definitely recognized—namely, that the human being is an individual because of and in relations with others.—*Ibid*.

3. Society has become in fact corporate. Its interests and activities are so tied together that human beings have become dependent upon one another, for good or for harm, to an unprecedented degree. This is a statement of fact, whether the fact be welcomed or deplored. This interdependence is increasing, not lessening. It must be taken into account by education. We must not only educate individuals to live in a world where social conditions beyond the reach of any one individual will affect his security, his work, his achievements, but we must take account of the total incapacity of the doctrine of competi-

tive individualism to work anything but harm in the state of interdependence in which we live. . .

The interdependence spoken of has developed on a world-wide scale. Isolated and excessive nationalism renders international interdependence, now existing as a fact, a source of fear, suspicion, antagonism, potential war. In order that interdependence may become a benefit instead of a dread evil and possible world-wide catastrophe, education must revise the conception of patriotism and good citizenship so that it will accord with the imperative demands of world-wide association and interaction.—In *The Educational Frontier* (with J. L. Childs; a Symposium, ed. by W. H. Kilpatrick).

4. Physical interdependence has increased beyond anything that could have been foreseen. . . The career of individuals, their lives and security as well as prosperity, is now affected by events on the other side of the world. The forces back of these events he cannot touch or influence—save perhaps by joining in a war of nations against nations. For we seem to live in a world in which nations try to deal with the problems created by the new situation by drawing more and more into themselves, by more and more extreme assertions of independent nationalist sovereignty, while everything they do in the direction of autarchy leads to ever closer mixture with other nations —but in war. . . The necessity of transforming physical interdependence into moral—into human—interdependence is part of the democratic problem.—*Freedom and Culture.*

See also: Conduct; Culture 1, 3; Dreams 2; Environment 3, 5; Experience 7; Law of Nature 4; Life 2;Morality 1; Order.

INTEREST

1. When things have to be *made* interesting it is because interest itself is wanting.—"Interest as Related to Will," in the Second Supplement to the *Herbart Year Book* for 1895.

2. Interest is normal and reliance upon it educationally legitimate in the degree in which the activity in question involves growth or development. Interest is illegitimate used in the degree in which it is either a symptom or a cause of arrested development in an activity.—*Interest and Effort in Education.*

See also: Democracy 3; Methods of Instruction 1; Peace; Society 2; Teaching 4, 5.

INTERNATIONAL RELATIONS

1. The situation that exists among nations in their relations to one another is such that it tempts even those who ordinarily come far short of cynicism to say that there is no connection between ethics and international relations.—*Characters and Events.*

2. Until nations are bound together by the law of a social order, there cannot be any truly moral obligations existing among them.—*Ibid.,* II.

J

JUDGMENT

1. The judgment when formed is a decision.—*How We Think*.

2. A man of good judgment in a given set of affairs is a man in so far educated, trained, whatever may be his literacy. And if our schools turn out their pupils in that attitude of mind which is conducive to good judgment in any department of affairs in which the pupils are placed, they have done more than if they sent out their pupils merely possessed of vast stores of information, or high degrees of skill in specialized branches. —*Ibid*.

See also: Criticism; Interaction 2; Thinking 11; Value 2, 5.

JUSTICE

Justice is a privilege which falls to a man as belonging to some group—not otherwise. The member of the clan or the household or the village community has a claim, but the stranger has no standing. He may be treated kindly, as a guest, but he cannot demand "justice" at the hands of any group but his own. —*Ethics* (with J. H. Tufts).

See also: War 2.

K

KNOWLEDGE

1. Knowledge implies reference to the self or mind. Knowing is an intellectual process, involving psychical laws. It is an activity which the self experiences. A certain individual activity has been accordingly presupposed in all the universal facts of physical science. These facts are all facts known by some mind, and hence fall, in some way, within the sphere of psychology. This science is accordingly something more than one science by the side of others; it is a central science, for its subject-matter, knowledge, is involved in them all.—*Psychology*.

2. To find out how to make knowledge when it is needed is the true end of the acquisition of information in school, not the information itself.—*Schools of To-Morrow* (with Evelyn Dewey).

3. Information severed from thoughtful action is dead, a mind-crushing load. Since it simulates knowledge and thereby develops the poison of conceit, it is a most powerful obstacle to further growth in the grace of intelligence.—*Democracy and Education.*

4. Knowledge is always a matter of the use that is made of experienced natural events.—In the *Creative Intelligence*: Essays in the Pragmatic Attitude (a Symposium).

5. Knowledge is not something separate and self-sufficient, but is involved in the process in which life is sustained and evolved. The senses lose their place as gateways of knowing to take their rightful place as stimuli to action. To an animal an affection of the eye or ear is not an idle piece of information about something indifferently going on in the world. It is an invitation and inducement to act in a needed way. It is a clue in behavior, a directive factor in adaptation of life in its surroundings. It is urgent, not cognitive in quality.—*Reconstruction in Philosophy*.

6. Knowledge is power and knowledge is achieved by sending the mind to school of nature to learn her processes of change.—*Ibid.*

7. The reason a baby can know little and an experienced adult much when confronting the same things is not because the latter has a "mind" which the former has not, but because one has already formed habits which the other has still to acquire. The scientific man and the philosopher like the carpenter, the physician and politician know with their habits, not with their "consciousness."—*Human Nature and Conduct*.

8. Of course there has been an enormous increase in the amount of knowledge possessed by mankind, but it does not equal probably the increase in the amount of errors and half-truths which have got into circulation.—*The Public and Its Problems*.

9. Knowledge falters when imagination clips its wings or fears to use them. Every great advance in science has issued from a new audacity of imagination.—*The Quest for Certainty*.

10. Knowledge is a mode of practical action.—*Ibid.*

11. Acknowledgment that we do not know what we do not

know is a necessity of all intellectual integrity.—*A Common Faith.*

See also: Democracy 11; Experimental Method 1; Facts 2; Freedom 2; Hypotheses 1; Inference 1; Liberal Education; Machine 1; Mind 7; Open-mindedness 3; Philosophy 7; Possibility 1, 2; Thinking 3; Understanding 5; Wisdom 2.

L

LABOR

Labor means a form of work in which the direct result accomplished is of value only as a means of exchange for something else. It is an economic term, being applied to that form of work where the product is paid for, and the money paid is used for objects of more direct values.—*Interest and Effort in Education.*

See also: Economics; Production and Consumption 1, 2.

LANGUAGE

1. Language includes much more than oral and written speech, gestures, pictures, monuments, visual images, finger movements—anything consciously employed as a sign is, logically, language.—*How We Think.*

2. All language, all symbols, are implements of an indirect experience; in technical language the experience which is procured by their means is "mediated." It stands in contrast with an immediate, direct experience, something in which we take part vitally and at first hand, instead of through the intervention of representative media. . . Direct experience is very limited. If it were not for the intervention of agencies for

representing absent and distant affairs, our experience would remain almost on the level of that of the brutes. Every step from savagery to civilization is dependent upon the invention of media which enlarge the range of purely immediate experience.—*Democracy and Education*.

3. Language exists only when it is listened to as well as spoken. The hearer is an indispensable partner.—*Art as Experience*.

4. Language comes infinitely short of paralleling the variegated surface of nature. Yet words as practical devices are the agencies by which the ineffable diversity of natural existence as it operates in human experience is reduced to orders, ranks, and classes that can be managed. Not only is it impossible that language should duplicate the infinite variety of individualized qualities that exist, but it is wholly undesirable and unneeded that it should do so. The unique quality of a quality is found in experience itself; it is there and sufficiently there not to need reduplication in language. The latter serves its scientific or its intellectual purpose as it gives directions as to how to come upon these qualities in experience. The more generalized and simple the direction the better.—*Ibid*.

See also: Art 2; Children 2; Interaction 2; Mathematics 3; Mind 1; Speech 2.

LAW

1. Now it is true that . . . laws are made by man rather than that man is made for them.—*Reconstruction in Philosophy*.

2. Law is one of the most conservative of human institutions; yet through the cumulative effect of legislation and judicial decisions it changes, sometimes at a slow rate, sometimes rapidly. The changes in human relations that are brought about by changes in industrial and legal institutions then react to modify the ways in which human nature manifests itself, and this

brings about still further changes in institutions, and so on indefinitely.—*Problems of Men.*

See also: Judgment; Ideals 1; International Relations 2.

LAW OF NATURE

1. The notion that laws govern and forces rule is an animistic survival. It is a product of reading nature in terms of politics in order to turn around and then read politics in the light of supposed sanctions of nature.—*The Influence of Darwin on Philosophy and Other Essays.*

2. The notion of law changes. It is no longer something governing things and events from on high; it is the statement of their own order.—*Essays in Experimental Logic.*

3. The idea of a universal reign of law, based on properties immutably inhering in things and of such a nature as to be capable of exact mathematical statement, was a sublime idea. It displaced once for all the notion of a world in which the unaccountable and the mysterious have the first and last word, a world in which they constantly insert themselves. It established the ideal of regularity and uniformity in place of the casual and sporadic. It gave men inspiration and guidance in seeking for uniformities and constancies where only irregular diversity was experienced. The ideal extended itself from the inanimate world to the animate and then to social affairs. It became, it may fairly be said, the great article of faith in the creed of scientific men.—*The Quest for Certainty.*

4. Laws are inherently conceptual in character, as is shown in the fact that either position or velocity may be fixed at will. To call them conceptual is not to say that they are merely "mental" or arbitrary. It is to say that they are relations which are thought, not observed. The subject-matter of the conceptions which constitute laws is not arbitrary, for it is determined by the interactions of what exists.—*Ibid.*

5. The aim of science is law. A law is adequate in the degree in which it takes the form, if not of an equation, at least of formulation of constancy, of relationship, or order. It is clear that any law, whether stated as formulation of order or as an equation, conveys, in and of itself, not an individualized reality, but a certain connection of conditions.—*Problems of Men.*

See also: Nature 1.

LEADERSHIP

The world has suffered more from leaders and authorities than from the masses.—*The Public and Its Problems.*

See also: Democracy 10.

LEARNING

1. The first years of learning proceed rapidly and securely before children go to school, because that learning is so closely related with the motives that are furnished by their own powers and the needs that are dictated by their own conditions. . . If we want, then, to find out how education takes place most successfully, let us go to the experiences of children where learning is a necessity, and not to the practices of the schools where it is largely an adornment, a superfluity and even an unwelcome imposition.—*Schools of To-Morrow* (with Evelyn Dewey).

2. As civilization advances, the gap between the capacities of the young and the concerns of adults widens. Learning by direct sharing in the pursuits of adults becomes increasingly difficult. Intentional agencies—schools—and explicit materials —studies—are devised. The task of teaching certain things is delegated to a special group of persons.—*Democracy and Education.*

See also: Methods of Instruction 2; School 4, 8; Teaching 3, 4; Thinking 10.

LEISURE

The rigid identification of work with material interests and leisure with ideal interests is itself a social product.—*Democracy and Education.*

See also: Production and Consumption 2; Theory 2; Work 2.

LIBERAL EDUCATION

#1 Liberal education aims to train intelligence for its proper office: to know.—*Democracy and Education.*

LIBERALISM

1. The slogans of the liberalism of one period often become the bulwarks of reaction in a subsequent era.—*Philosophy and Civilization.*

2. Liberalism is committed to an end that is at once enduring and flexible: the liberation of individuals so that realization of their capacities may be the law of their life. . . Liberalism has to assume the responsibility for making it clear that intelligence is a social asset and is clothed with a function as public as is its origin, in the concrete, in social cooperation.—*Liberalism and Social Action.*

3. The meaning of liberalism has undergone many changes since the word came into vogue not very much more than a century ago. The word came into use to denote a new spirit that grew and spread with the rise of democracy. It implied a new interest in the common man and a new sense that the common man, the representative of the great masses of human beings, had possibilities that had been kept under, that had not been allowed to develop, because of institutional and political conditions. This new spirit was liberal in both senses of the word. It was marked by a generous attitude, by sympathy for the underdog, for those who were not given a chance. It was part of a wide-spread rise of humanitarian philanthropy. It was

75

also liberal in that it aimed at enlarging the scope of free action on the part of those who for ages had had no part in public affairs and no lot in the benefits secured by this participation.— *Problems of Men.*

4. Liberalism knows that an individual is nothing fixed, given, ready-made. It is something achieved, and achieved not in isolation, but with the aid and support of conditions, cultural and physical, including "cultural" economic, legal and political institutions as well as science and art. Liberalism knows that social conditions may restrict, distort and almost prevent the development of individuality. It therefore takes an active interest in the working of social institutions that have a bearing, positive or negative, upon the growth of individuals who shall be rugged in fact and not merely in abstract theory. It is as much interested in the positive construction of favorable institutions, legal, political and economic, as it is in the work of removing abuses and overt oppressions.

In the second place, liberalism is committed to the idea of historic relativity. It knows that the content of the individual and freedom change with time; that this is as true of social change as it is of individual development from infancy to maturity. The positive counterpart of opposition to doctrinal absolutism is experimentalism. The connection between historic relativity and experimental method is intrinsic. Time signifies change. The significance of individuality with respect to social policies alters with change of the conditions in which individuals live...

The commitment of liberalism to experimental procedure carries with it the idea of continuous reconstruction of the ideas of individuality and of liberty in intimate connection with changes in social relations. It is enough to refer to the changes in productivity and distribution since the time when the earlier liberalism was formulated, and the effect of these transformations, due to science and technology, upon the terms on which men associate together. An experimental method is the recognition of this temporal change in ideas and policies so that the latter shall coordinate with the facts instead of being opposed to them...

The two things essential, then, to thorough-going social liberalism are, first, realistic study of existing conditions in their movement, and, secondly, leading ideas, in the form of policies for dealing with these conditions in the interest of development of increased individuality and liberty.—*Ibid*.

See also: Freedom 4.

LIBERTY

1. Liberty is tolerated as long as it does not seem to menace in any way the status quo of society.—*Liberalism and Social Action*.

2. Liberty is not just an idea, an abstract principle. It is power, effective power to do specific things.—"Liberty and Social Control," in the *Social Frontier*, II (1935).

3. Will men surrender their liberties if they believe that by so doing they will obtain the satisfaction that comes from a sense of fusion with others and that respect by others which is the product of the strength furnished by solidarity?—*Freedom and Culture*.

4. There is no such thing as liberty in general; liberty, so to speak, at large. If one wants to know what the condition of liberty is at a given time, one has to examine what persons can do and what they cannot do. The moment one examines the question from the standpoint of effective action, it becomes evident that the demand for liberty is a demand for power, either for possession of powers of action not already possessed or for retention and expansion of powers already possessed.—*Problems of Men*.

5. Liberty is a social matter and not just a claim of the private individual.—*Ibid.*

See also: Freedom 6; Right 3; Security 2; War 2.

LIFE

1. Empirically speaking, the most obvious difference between living and non-living things is that the activities of the former are characterized by needs, by efforts which are active demands to satisfy needs, and by satisfactions.—*Experience and Nature.*

2. Life goes on in an environment; not merely in it but because of it, through interaction with it. No creature lives merely under the skin; its subcutaneous organs are means of connection with what lies beyond its bodily frame, and to which, in order to live, it must adjust itself, by accommodation and defense but also by conquest. At every moment, the living creature is exposed to dangers from its surroundings, and at every moment, it must draw upon something in its surroundings to satisfy its needs. The career and destiny of a living being are bound up with its interchanges with its environment, not externally but in the most intimate way.—*Art as Experience.*

3. The means by which we make a living should be transformed into ways of making a life that is worth the living.— Reply in *The Philosophy of John Dewey* (a Symposium, ed. by P. A. Schilpp).

4. No form of life does or can stand still; it either goes forward or it goes backward, and the end of the backward road is death.—*Problems of Men.*

See also: Education 2; Environment 3; Experience 2; Growth 1; Knowledge 5; Society 1.

LOGIC

1. Logic is both a science and an art; a science so far as it gives an organized and tested descriptive account of the way

in which thought actually goes on; an art, so far as on the basis of this description it projects methods by which future thinking shall take advantage of the operations that lead to success and avoid those which result in failure.—*Reconstruction in Philosophy.*

2. Man is not logical and his intellectual history is a record of mental reserves and compromises. He hangs on to what he can in his old beliefs even when he is compelled to surrender their logical basis.—*Human Nature and Conduct.*

See also: Mathematics 2; Philosophy 8; Possibility 2.

LOYALTY

1. Loyalty to whatever in the established environment makes a life of excellence possible is the beginning of all progress.—*Human Nature and Conduct.*

2. The loyalties which once held individuals, which gave them support, direction, and unity of outlook on life, have well-nigh disappeared. In consequence, individuals are confused and bewildered. It would be difficult to find in history an epoch as lacking as is the present. Stability of individuality is dependent upon stable objects to which allegiance firmly attaches itself.—*Individualism, Old and New.*

M

MACHINE

1. Machines depend in their action upon complicated facts and principles of nature which are not recognized by the worker unless he has had special intellectual training. The machine worker, unlike the older hand worker, is following blindly the intelligence of others instead of his own knowledge of materials, tools, and processes.—*Schools of To-Morrow* (with Evelyn Dewey).

2. A machine age is a challenge to generate new conceptions of the ideal and the spiritual.—*Individualism, Old and New.*

3. Machinery means an undreamed-of reservoir of power. If we have harnessed this power to the dollar rather than to the liberation and enrichment of human life, it is because we have been content to stay within the bounds of traditional aims and values.—*Ibid.*

See also: Facts 2; World 2.

MAN

1. Man differs from the lower animals because he preserves his past experience. What happens in the past is lived again in memory. About what goes on today hangs a cloud of thoughts concerning similar things undergone in bygone days. With the

animals, an experience perishes as it happens, and each new doing or suffering stands alone. But man lives in a world where each occurrence is charged with echoes and reminiscences of what has gone before, where each event is a reminder of other things.—*Reconstruction in Philosophy*.

2. Man, a child in understanding of himself, has placed in his hands physical tools of incalculable power. He plays with them like a child.—*The Public and Its Problems*.

3. While man is other than bird and beast, he shares basic vital functions with them and has to make the same basal adjustments if he is to continue the process of living. Having the same vital needs, man derives the means by which he breathes, moves, looks and listens, the very brain with which he coordinates his senses and his movements, from his animal forbears. The organs with which he maintains himself in being are not of himself alone, but by grace of struggles and achievements of a long line of animal ancestry.—*Art as Experience*.

See also: Environment 5; Evolution; Law 1; State 1.

MANNERS
Manners are but minor morals.—*Democracy and Education*.

MATHEMATICS
1. Mathematical ideas are indispensable instruments of physical research, and no account of the method of the latter is complete that does not take into account the applicability of mathematical conceptions to natural existence.—*The Quest for Certainty*.

2. Within mathematical science, symbols are individual objects of just the same logical nature as are metals and acids in chemistry and as are rocks and fossils in geology.—*Problems of Men*.

3. Mathematics is a highly developed language; like language, it is fruitfully applicable in our dealings with the world,

but no more than any other language is it a part of that world save as man himself is part of it.—In the *Humanist,* VII.

See also: Law of Nature 3; Matter 3; Nature 1; Objects 2.

MATTER

1. The notion of matter actually found in the practice of science has nothing in common with the matter of materialists. —*Experience and Nature.*

2. I fail to see what meaning "matter" and "materialism" have for philosophy. Matter has a definite assignable meaning in physical science. It designates something capable of being expressed in mathematical symbols which are distinguished from those defining energy. It is not possible to generalize the definite meaning "matter" has in this context of physical science into a philosophical view—which materialism most definitely is.—Reply in *The Philosophy of John Dewey* (a Symposium, ed. by P. A. Schilpp).

3. "Matter" has in modern science none of the low, base, inert properties assigned to it in classic Greek and medieval philosophy, properties that were the ground for setting it in stark opposition to all that is higher. . . It would be difficult to find a greater distance between any two terms than that which separates "matter" in the Greek-medieval tradition and the technical signification, suitably expressed in mathematical symbols, that the word bears in science today.—"Antinaturalism in Extremis," in *Naturalism and the Human Spirit* (a Symposium, ed. by Y. H. Krikorian).

MEMORY

Memory is vicarious experience in which there is all the emotional value of actual experience without its strains, vicissitudes and troubles.—*Reconstruction in Philosophy.*

See also: Man 1.

METHODS OF INSTRUCTION

1. The question of method is ultimately reducible to the question of order or development of the child's powers and interests. —*My Pedagogic Creed.*

2. Existing methods of instruction give plenty of evidence in support of a belief that minds are opposed to learning—to their own exercise. We fail to see that such aversion is in reality a condemnation of our methods; a sign that we are presenting material for which the mind in its existing state of growth has no need, or else presenting it in such ways as to cover up the real need.—*Schools of To-Morrow* (with Evelyn Dewey).

See also: School 2.

MIND

1. Mind has not remained a passive spectator of the universe, but has produced and is producing certain results. These results are objective, can be studied as all objective historical facts may be, and are permanent. They are the most fixed, certain, and universal signs to us of the way in which mind works. Such objective manifestations of mind are, in the realm of intelligence, phenomena like language and science; in that of will, social and political institutions; in that of feeling, art; in that of the whole self, religion.—*Psychology.*

2. I am not aware of any so-called merely "mental" activity or result that cannot be described in the objective terms of organic activity modified and directed by symbols-meaning, or language, in its broad sense.—*How We Think.*

3. Mind denotes the whole system of meanings as they are embodied in the workings of organic life; consciousness in a being with language denotes awareness or perception of meanings; it is the perception of actual events, whether past, contemporary, or future, in their meanings, the having of actual ideas. The greater part of mind is only implicit in any con-

scious act or stare; the field of mind—of operative meanings—is enormously wider than that of consciousness. Mind is contextual and persistent; consciousness is focal and transitive. Mind is, so to speak, structural, substantial; a constant background and foreground; perceptive consciousness is process, a series of heres and nows. Mind is a constant luminosity; consciousness intermittent, a series of flashes of varying intensities. Consciousness is, as it were, the occasional interception of messages continually transmitted, as a mechanical receiving device selects a few of the vibrations with which the air is filled and renders them audible.—*Experience and Nature.*

4. A mind that has opened itself to experience and that has ripened through its discipline knows its own littleness and impotencies; it knows that its wishes and acknowledgments are not final measures of the universe whether in knowledge or in conduct, and hence are, in the end, transient. But it also knows that its juvenile assumption of power and achievement is not a dream to be wholly forgotten. It implies a unity with the universe that is to be preserved. The belief, and the effort of thought and struggle which it inspires, are also the doing of the universe, and they in some way, however slight, carry the universe forward. A chastened sense of our importance, apprehension that it is not a yardstick by which to measure the whole, is consistent with the belief that we and our endeavors are significant not only for themselves but in the whole.—*Experience and Nature.*

5. Mind is no longer a spectator beholding the world from without and finding its highest satisfaction in the joy of self-sufficing contemplation. The mind is within the world as a part of the latter's own ongoing process. It is marked off as mind by the fact that wherever it is found, changes take place in a directed way, so that a movement in a definite one-way sense—from the doubtful and confused to the clear, resolved and settled —takes place.—*The Quest for Certainty.*

6. Mind is more than consciousness, because it is the abiding even though changing background of which consciousness is the foreground. Mind changes slowly through the joint tuition of interest and circumstance. Consciousness is always in rapid change, for it marks the place where the formed disposition and the immediate situation touch and interact. It is the continuous readjustment of self and the world in experience.—*Art as Experience*.

7. "Minds" exist and do the knowing.—*Knowing and the Known* (with A. F. Bentley).

See also: Conservatism 3; Inference 2; Interaction 1; Knowledge 1, 6, 7; Open-mindedness 1, 3; Philosophy 7; Responsibility 3; Social Psychology.

MISTAKES

The great thing is not to avoid mistakes but to have them take place under conditions such that they can be utilized to increase intelligence in the future.—*Reconstruction in Philosophy*.

See also: Knowledge 8; Science 1; Thinking 8.

MONEY

1. We do not eat money, or wear it, or marry it, or listen for musical strains to issue from it. . . . Pecuniary profit in itself, in other words, is always strictly instrumental, and it is of the nature of this instrument to be effective in proportion to size.—*Human Nature and Conduct*.

2. Anthropologically speaking, we are living in a money culture. . . . Our materialism, our devotion to money making and to having a good time, are not things by themselves. They are the product of the fact that we live in a money culture; of the fact that our technique and technology are controlled by interest in private profit.—*Individual, Old and New*.

3. Money spent on education is a social investment—an investment in future well-being, moral, economic, physical, and intellectual, of the country.—"Crisis in Education," in *The American Teacher*, XVII (1933).

See also: Culture 3; Labor; Morality 1.

MORALITY

1. Morals is as much a matter of interaction of a person with his social environment as walking is an interaction of legs with a physical environment. The character of walking depends upon the strength and competency of legs. But it also depends upon whether a man is walking in a bog or on a paved street, upon whether there is a safeguarded path set aside or whether he has to walk amid dangerous vehicles. If the standard of morals is low it is because the education given by the interaction of the individual with his social environment is defective. Of what avail is it to preach unassuming simplicity and contentment of life when communal admiration goes to the man who "succeeds"—who makes himself conspicuous and envied because of command of money and other forms of power?—*Human Nature and Conduct.*

2. Morals has to do with all activity into which alternative possibilities enter. For wherever they enter a difference between better and worse arises. Reflection upon action means uncertainty and consequent need of decision as to which course is better.—*Ibid.*

3. All moral judgment is experimental and subject to revision.—*Ibid.*

4. Why did morality set up rules so foreign to human nature? —*Human Nature and Conduct.*

5. Morals may be a growing science if it is to be a science at all, not merely because all truth has not yet been appropriated

by the mind of man, but because life is a moving affair in which old moral truth ceases to apply.—*Ibid.*

6. Morals is not a theme by itself because it is not an episode nor department by itself. It marks the issue of all the converging forces of life.—"Credo," in the *Living Philosophies* (a Symposium).

7. When social life is in a state of flux, moral issues cease to gather exclusively about personal conformity and deviation. They center in the value of social arrangements, of laws, of inherited traditions that have crystallized into institutions, in changes that are desirable. Institutions lose their quasi-sacredness and are the objects of moral questioning. We now live in such a period.—*Ethics* (with J. H. Tufts; revised ed.).

8. Just as physical life cannot exist without the support of a physical environment, so moral life cannot go on without the support of a moral environment.—*Art as Experience.*

See also: Discussion 2; International Relations 2; Perfection.

MORAL SCIENCE

Morals is the most humane of all subjects. It is that which is closest to human nature; it is ineradicably empirical, not theological nor metaphysical nor mathematical. Since it directly concerns human nature, everything that can be known of the human mind and body in physiology, medicine, anthropology, and psychology is pertinent to moral inquiry. Human nature exists and operates in an environment. And it is not "in" that environment as coins are in a box, but as a plant is in the sunlight and soil. It is of them, continuous with their energies, dependent upon their support, capable of increase only as it utilizes them, and as it gradually rebuilds from their crude indifference an environment genially civilized. Hence physics, chemistry, history, statistics, engineering, science, are a part of disciplined moral knowledge so far as they enable us to understand the conditions and agencies through which man lives, and on account of which he forms and executes his plans. Moral science is not something with a separate province. It is physical, biological and historic knowledge placed in a human context where it will illuminate and guide the activities of men. —*Human Nature and Conduct.*

See also: Morality.

N

NATURALISM

1. The naturalistic method, when it is consistently followed, destroys many things once cherished; but it destroys them by revealing their inconsistency with the nature of things—a flaw that always attended them and deprived them of efficacy for aught save emotional consolation. But its main purport is not destructive; empirical naturalism is rather a winnowing fan.— *Experience and Nature.*

2. Philosophic naturalism still has a work to do in a field that so far it has hardly done more than touch. . . . Such words as "mind," "subject," "self," "person," "the individual," to say nothing of "value," are more than tinged in their current usage with signification they absorbed from beliefs of an extranatural character. There is almost no word employed in psychological and societal analysis and description that does not reflect this influence.—"Antinaturalism in Extremis," in *Naturalism and the Human Spirit* (a Symposium, ed. by Y. H. Krikorian).

NATURE

1. Nature is not an unchangeable order, unwinding itself majestically from the reel of law under the control of deified forces. It is an indefinite congeries of changes. Laws are not

governmental regulations which limit change, but are convenient formulations of selected portions of change followed through a longer or shorter period of time, and then registered in statistical forms that are amenable to mathematical manipulation.—*The Influence of Darwin on Philosophy and Other Essays.*

2. Man's home is nature; his purposes and aims are dependent for execution upon natural conditions. Separated from such conditions they become empty dreams and idle indulgences of fancy.—*Democracy and Education.*

3. Nature has no preference for good things over bad things, its mills turn out any kind of grist indifferently.—*Experience and Nature.*

4. The human situation falls wholly within nature. It reflects the traits of nature, it gives indisputable evidence that in nature itself qualities and relations, individualities and uniformities, finalities and efficacies, contingencies and necessities are inextricably bound together.—*Ibid.*

5. Nature is capable of being understood. . . . Nature has intelligible order as its possession in the degree in which we by our own overt operations realize potentialities contained in it. —*The Quest for Certainty.*

See also: Experience 4; Knowledge 6; Law of Nature 1; Order; Power 2.

O

OBEDIENCE

Parents, priests, chiefs, social censors have supplied aims, aims which were foreign to those upon whom they were imposed, to the young, laymen, ordinary folk; a few have given and administered rule, and the mass have in a passable fashion and with reluctance obeyed. Everybody knows that good children are those who make as little trouble as possible for their elders, and since most of them cause a good deal of annoyance they must be naughty by nature. Generally speaking, good people have been those who did what they were told to do, and lack of eager compliance is a sign of something wrong in their nature.—*Human Nature and Conduct.*

See also: Discipline 2.

OBJECTIVITY

The condition either of total lack of interest or of impartially distributed interest is as mythical as the story of the ass in scholastic ethics.*—*Interest and Effort in Education.*

See also: Mind 1; Philosophers 1.

* The story attributed to a fourteenth century thinker by the name of Buridan states that an ass, once placed precisely between two identical mangers, would perish from starvation, being completely unable to decide from which manger to start eating.

OBJECTS

1. The proper objects of science are nature.—*Experience and Nature.*

2. It is not a new discovery that the word "object" is highly ambiguous, being used for the sticks and stones, the cats and dogs, the chairs and tables of ordinary experiences, for the atoms and electrons of physics, and for any kind of "entity" that has logical subsistence—as in mathematics. In spite of the recognized ambiguity, one whole branch of modern epistemology is derived from the assumption that in the case of at least the first two cases, the word "object" has the same general meaning. For otherwise the subject-matter of physics and the things of everyday experience would not have presented themselves as rivals, and philosophy would not have felt an obligation to decide which is "real" and which is "appearance," or at least an obligation to set up a scheme in which they are "reconciled." The place occupied in modern philosophy by the problem of the relation of the so-called "scientific objects" and "common-sense objects" is proof, in any case, of the dominating presence of a distinction between the "objective" and the "subjective" which was unknown in ancient philosophy. It indicates that at least in the sense of awareness of an ever-present problem, modern philosophy is "objective-subjective," not just subjective....

Genuinely complete empirical philosophy requires that there be a determination in terms of experience of the relation that exists between physical subject-matter and the things of direct perception, use, and enjoyment. It would seem clear that historic empiricism, because of its commitment to sensationalism, failed to meet this need. The obvious way of meeting the requirement is through explicit acknowledgment that direct experience contains, as a highly important direct ingredient of itself, a wealth of *possible* objects. There is no inconsistency between the idea of direct experience and the idea of objects of that experience which are as yet unrealized. For these latter objects are directly experienced as possibilities. Every plan, every protection, yes, every forecast and anticipation, is an experience in which some non-directly experienced object is directly experienced *as a possibility*. And, as previously suggested, modern experience is marked by the extent to which directly perceived, enjoyed, and suffered objects are treated as signs, indications of what has not been experienced in and of itself, or/and are treated as means for the realization of these things of possible experience. Because historic empirical philosophy failed to take cognizance of this fact, it was not able to account for one of the most striking features of scientific method and scientific conclusions—preoccupation with generality as such.

For scientific methods and scientific subject-matter combine highly abstract or "theoretical" considerations with directly present concrete sensible material, and the generality of conclusions reached is directly dependent upon the presence of the first-named type of considerations. Now in modern philosophy, just as scientific "objects" have been set over against objects in direct experience, thereby occasioning the ontological problem of modern philosophy (the problem of where "reality" is to be found), so identification of the experiential with but one of the two factors of the method of knowing has created the epistemological problem of modern philosophy: the relation of the "conceptual" and "perceptual"; of sense and understanding.—*Problems of Men*.

See also: Art 3; Desire 1; Possibility 2.

OPEN-MINDEDNESS

1. Openness of mind means accessibility of mind to any and every consideration that will throw light upon the situation that needs to be cleared up, and that will help determine the

consequences of acting this way or that.—*Democracy and Education.*

2. Open-mindedness is very different from empty-mindedness. While it is hospitality to new themes, facts, ideas, questions, it is not the kind of hospitality that would be indicated by hanging out a sign: "Come right in; there is nobody at home." It includes an active desire to listen to more sides than one; to give heed to facts from whatever source they come; to give full attention to alternative possibilities; to recognize the possibility of error even in the beliefs that are dearest to us.— *How to Think.*

3. The open mind is a nuisance if it is merely passively open to allow anything to find its way into a vacuous mind behind the opening. It is significant only as it is the mark of an actively searching mind, one on the alert for further knowledge and understanding.—*Education and the Social Order* (a Pamphlet). *See also*: Ignorance.

OPTIMISM

The optimism that says that the world is already the best possible of all worlds might be regarded as the most cynical of pessimisms. If this is the best possible, what would a world which was fundamentally bad be like?—*Reconstruction in Philosophy.*

ORDER

There is in nature, even below the level of life, something more than mere flux and change. . . . Changes interlock and sustain each other. Wherever there is coherence, there is endurance. Order is not imposed from without but is made out of the relations of harmonious interactions that energies bear to one another. . . . Order cannot but be admirable in a world constantly threatened with disorder—in a world where living creatures can go on living only by taking advantage of whatever order exists about them, incorporating it into themselves. —*Art as Experience.*

See also: International Relations 2; Law of Nature 2; Nature 1, 5.

P

PEACE

Our country has been favored above other nations in its geographical position and by its history. Our remoteness from the great warring countries, our size and our resources have for the most part protected us from the entanglements, the jealousies, suspicions and animosities which the long, sad centuries have decreed to Europe. With such conditions it would be a shame indeed if a spirit of good-will, a spirit of amity to other nations, had not grown up among us. . . . We have, to be sure, an economic interest in the peace of the world, since peaceful and industrial nations make the best and safest customers. I would not belittle any motive that tends toward peace. But we have an interest in the peace of the world deeper and broader than that which self-interest dictates. We are bound by the history and spirit of our position in the world, and the law of *noblesse oblige*—the law that urges that every human being shall use his advantages and privileges not for his own enjoyment alone, but as well for the aid and service of his neighbors—lies more heavily upon us than it does upon any other nation that has ever existed. If we should be recreant to the trust we prove ourselves unworthy of our past and of our opportunity.—*Characters and Events*, II.

See also: Certainty 2; War 3.

PERCEPTION

1. The visible is set in the invisible; and in the end what is unseen decides what happens in the seen; the tangible rests precariously upon the untouched and ungrasped.—*Experience and Nature.*

2. We speak of perception *and* its object. But perception and its object are built up and complete in one and the same continuing operation.—*Art as Experience.*

See also: Culture 2; Mind 3; Objects 2.

PERFECTION

Not perfection as a final goal, but the ever enduring process of perfecting, maturing, refining, is the aim of living. . . . The bad man is the man who, no matter how good he has been, is beginning to deteriorate, to grow less good. The good man is the man who, no matter how morally unworthy he has been, is moving to become better. Such a conception makes one severe in judging himself and humane in judging others. *Reconstruction in Philosophy.*

See also: Possibility 4.

PHILOSOPHERS

1. As the philosopher has received his problem from the world of action, so he must return his account there for auditing and liquidation.—*The Influence of Darwin on Philosophy and Other Essays.*

2. It is an old story that philosophers, in common with theologians and social theorists, are as sure that personal habits and interests shape their opponents' doctrines as they are that their own beliefs are "absolutely" universal and objective in quality. —*Essays in Experimental Logic.*

3. Philosophy recovers itself when it ceases to be a device for dealing with the problems of philosophers and becomes a

method, cultivated by philosophers, for dealing with the problems of men.—In the *Creative Intelligence: Essays in the Pragmatic Attitude* (a Symposium).

4. Philosophers are parts of history, caught in its movement; creators perhaps in some measure of its future, but also assuredly creatures of its past.—*Philosophy and Civilization.*

5. A philosopher who would relate his thinking to present civilization, in its predominantly technological and industrial character, cannot ignore any of [the past] movements. . . If he ignores traditions, his thoughts become thin and empty. But they are something to be employed, not just treated with respect or dressed out in a new vocabulary.—In *Whither Mankind* (ed. by C. A. Beard).

See also: Ideals 2; Philosophy; Pluralism; Possibility 2.

PHILOSOPHY

1. Better it is for philosophy to err in active participation in the living struggles and issues of its own age and time than to maintain an immune, monastic impeccability.—In the *Essays, Philosophical and Psychological, in Honor of William James* (a Symposium).

2. Philosophic theory has no Aladdin's lamp to summon into immediate existence the values which it intellectually constructs.—*Democracy and Education.*

3. When it is understood that philosophic thinking is caught up in the actual course of events, having the office of guiding them towards a prosperous issue, problems will abundantly present themselves. Philosophy will not solve these problems; philosophy is vision, imagination, reflection—and these functions apart from action, modify nothing and hence resolve nothing. But in a complicated and perverse world, action which is not informed with vision, imagination and reflection is more likely to increase confusion and conflict than to straighten things

out. In the *Creative Intelligence*: Essays in the Pragmatic Attitude (a Symposium).

4. Philosophy in America will be lost between chewing a historic cud long since reduced to woody fiber, or an apologetics for lost causes (lost to natural science), or a scholastic, schematic, formalism, unless it can somehow bring to consciousness America's own need and its own implicit principle of successful action.—*Ibid.*

5. What philosophy has been unconsciously, without knowing it or intending it, and, so to speak, under cover, it must henceforth be openly and deliberately. When it is acknowledged that, under disguise of dealing with ultimate reality, philosophy has been occupied with the precious values embedded in social traditions, that it has sprung from a clash of social ends and from a conflict of inherited institutions with incompatible contemporary tendencies, it will be seen that the task of future philosophy is to clarify men's ideas as to the social and moral strifes of their own day. Its aim is to become so far as is humanly possible an organ for dealing with these conflicts.—*Reconstruction in Philosophy.*

6. The distinctive office, problems and subject-matter of philosophy grow out of stresses and strains in the community life in which a given form of philosophy arises, and accordingly its specific problems vary with the changes in human life that are always going on and that at times constitute a crisis and a turning point in human history...

In philosophy today there are not many who exhibit confidence about its ability to deal competently with the serious issues of the day. Lack of confidence is manifested in concern for the improvement of techniques, and in threshing over the systems of the past. Both of these interests are justifiable in a way. But with respect to the first, the way of reconstruction is not through giving attention to form at the expense of substantial content, as in the case with techniques that are used only to develop and refine still more purely formal skills. With respect to the second, the way is not through increase of erudite scholarship about the past that throws no light upon the issues now troubling mankind. It is not too much to say that, as far as interest in the two topics just mentioned predominates, the withdrawal from the present scene, increasingly evident in philosophy, is itself a sign of the extent of the disturbance and unsettlement that now marks the other aspects of man's life. Indeed, we may go farther and say that such withdrawal is one manifestation of just those defects of past systems that render them of little value for the troubled affairs of the present: namely, the desire to find something so fixed and certain as to provide a secure refuge. The problems with which a philosophy relevant to the present must deal are those growing out of changes going on with ever-increasing rapidity, over an ever-increasing human-geographical range, and with ever-deepening intensity of penetration.—Introduction to the 1948 edition of *Reconstruction in Philosophy.*

7. Modern philosophy, understanding by this term that which has been influenced by the rise of the newer natural science, has contained within itself an inner division. It has tried to combine acceptance of the conclusions of scientific inquiry as to the natural world with acceptance of doctrines about the nature of mind and knowledge which originated before there was such a thing as systematic experimental inquiry. Between the two there is an inherent incompatibility.—*The Quest for Certainty.*

8. Philosophy is not a special road to something alien to ordinary beliefs, knowledge, action, enjoyment, and suffering. It is rather a criticism, a critical viewing, of just these familiar things. It differs from other criticism only in trying to carry it further and to pursue it methodically. . . Men thought before there was logic, and they judged right and wrong, good and evil, before there was ethics. Before there was ever anything termed metaphysics men were familiar with distinctions of the

real and the unreal in experience, with the fact that processes whether of physical or human nature have results, and that expected and desired results often do not happen because some process has its path crossed by some other course of events. But there is confusion and conflict, ambiguity and inconsistency, in our experience of familiar objects and in our beliefs and aspirations relating to them. As soon as any one strives to introduce definiteness, clarity, and order on any broad scale, he enters the road that leads to philosophy.—*Construction and Criticism.*

9. It shows a deplorable deadness of imagination to suppose that philosophy will indefinitely revolve within the scope of the problems and systems that two thousand years of European history have bequeathed to us. . . A chief task of those who call themselves philosophers is to help get rid of the useless lumber that blocks our highways of thought, and strive to make straight and open the paths that lead to the future.—"From Absolutism to Experimentalism," in *Contemporary American Philosophy,* II (a Symposium, ed. by G. P. Adams and W. P. Montague).

10. Philosophy, like art, moves in the medium of imaginative mind.—*Art as Experience.*

11. Philosophy still has a work to do. It may gain a role for itself by turning to consideration of why it is that man is now so alienated from man. It may turn to the projection of large generous hypotheses which, if used as plans of action, will give intellectual direction to men in search for ways to make the world more one of worth and significance, more homelike, in fact. There is no phase of life, educational, economic, political, religious, in which inquiry may not aid in bringing to birth that world which Matthew Arnold rightly said was as yet unborn. Present-day philosophy cannot desire a better work than to engage in the act of midwifery that was assigned to it by Socrates twenty-five hundred years ago.—*Problems of Men.*

See also: Civilization 4; Matter 2; Objects 2; Philosophers; Science 7.

PLURALISM

What philosophers have got to do is to work out a fresh analysis of the relations between the one and the many. Our shrinking world presents that issue today in a thousand different forms. Pluralism is the greatest philosophical idea of our times. How are we going to make the most of the new values we set on variety, difference, and individuality—how are we going to realize their possibilities in every field, and at the same time not sacrifice that plurality to the cooperation we need so much? How can we bring things together as we must without losing sight of plurality? There is an intellectual problem for philosophers to get busy upon!—From the last *Lecture* to his graduate students, as recorded in "The Idea of Pluralism" by J. H. Randall, Jr.

POSSIBILITY

1. Possibilities are more important than what already exists, and knowledge of the latter counts only in its bearing upon possibilities.—"Progressive Education and the Science of Education," in *Progressive Education*, V (1928).

2. The relation between objects as known and objects with respect to value is that between the actual and the possible. "The actual" consists of given conditions; "the possible" denotes ends or consequences not now existing but which the actual may through its use bring into existence. The possible in respect to any given actual situation is thus an ideal for that situation. . . There are three ways of idealizing the world. There is idealization through purely intellectual and logical processes, in which reasoning alone attempts to prove that the world has characters that satisfy our highest aspirations. There are, again, moments

of intense emotional appreciation when, through a happy conjunction of the state of the self and of the surrounding world, the beauty and harmony of existence is disclosed in experiences which are the immediate consummation of all for which we long. Then there is an idealization through actions that are directed by thought, such as are manifested in the works of fine art and in all human relations perfected by loving care. The first path has been taken by many philosophers. The second while it lasts is the more engaging. It sets the measure of our ideas of possibilities that are to be realized by intelligent endeavour. But its objects depend upon fortune and are insecure. The third method represents the way of deliberate quest for security of the values that are enjoyed by grace of our happy moments.—*The Quest for Certainty.*

3. Possibilities are embodied in works of art that are not elsewhere actualized.—*Art as Experience.*

4. No one lives in a world in which he has found everything at all times perfect. If he understands the meaning of this fact he has learned to be alive to possibilities. The potential *better* will then be regarded as the good—and the only good—of any situation, a statement as applicable to scientific inquiry as to any moral matter.—Reply in *The Philosophy of John Dewey* (a Symposium, ed. by P. A. Schilpp).

See also: Future 4; Ideals 2; Liberalism 3; Objects 2; Pluralism; Thinking 12; Value.

POWER

1. The madness with which the gods afflict those whom they would destroy is precisely the temptation to use a temporary possession of strategic power so as to make that power permanent.—*Characters and Events.*

2. Human power over the physical energies of nature has immensely increased. In moral ideal, power of man over physi-

cal nature should be employed to reduce, to eliminate progressively, the power of man over man. By what means shall we prevent its use to effect new, more subtle, more powerful agencies of subjection of men to other men? Both the issue of war or peace between nations, and the future of economic relations for years and generations to come in contribution either to human freedom or human subjection are involved. An increase of power undreamed of a century ago, one to whose further increase no limits can be put as long as scientific inquiry goes on, is an established fact. The thing still uncertain is what we are going to do with it.—*Freedom and Culture.*

3. The possession of effective power is always a matter of the distribution of power that exists at the time. A physical analogy may make clear what I mean. Water runs downhill and electric currents flow because of difference in potentials. If the ground is level, water is stagnant. If on the level of ocean, there are dashing waves, it is because there is another power operating, that of the winds, occasioned ultimately by a difference in the distribution of temperature at different points. There is no such thing physically as manifestation of energy or effective power by one thing except in relation to the energy manifested by other things. There is no such thing as the liberty or effective power of an individual, group, or class, except in relations to the liberties, the effective powers, of other individuals, groups, and classes.

Demand for retention of powers already possessed on the part of a particular group means, therefore, that other individuals and groups shall continue to possess only the capacities in and for activity which they already possess. Demand for increased power at one point means demand for change in the distribution of powers, that is, for less power somewhere else. You cannot discuss or measure the liberty of one individual or group of individuals without thereby raising the question of the effect upon the liberty of others, any more than you can measure the energy of a head water at the head without measuring the difference of levels.—*Problems of Men.*

See also: Authority 2; Human Concerns; Knowledge 6; Liberty 4; Machine 3; Man 2.

PRAGMATISM

1. I . . . affirm that the term "pragmatic" means only the rule of referring all thinking, all reflective considerations, to consequences for final meaning and test.—*Essays in Experimental Logic.*

2. Pragmatism as attitude represents what Mr. Peirce has happily termed "the laboratory habit of mind" extended into every arena where inquiry may fruitfully be carried on.—*Ibid.*

See also: Reality 2.

PREJUDICE

Prejudice is strengthened in influence, but hardly in value, by the number who share it.—*Essays in Experimental Logic.*

See also: Psychology; School 6.

PRESENT AND PAST

1. "Present" activity is not a sharp narrow knife-blade in time. The present is complex, containing within itself a multitude of habits and impulses. It is enduring, a course of action, a process including memory, observation and foresight, a pressure forward, a glance backward and a look outward. It is of moral moment because it marks a transition in the direction of breadth and clarity of action or in that of triviality and confusion.—*Human Nature and Conduct.*

2. Knowledge of the past is significant only as it deepens and extends our understanding of the present.—*Logic: the Theory of Inquiry.*

See also: Change 5; Education 15; Future 2, 4; History 1; Philosophers 4; Progress 2.

PROBLEMS

1. Problems are solved only where they arise—namely in action, in the adjustments of behavior. But, for good or for evil, they can be solved only with method; and ultimately method is intelligence, and intelligence is method.—*The Influence of Darwin on Philosophy and Other Essays.*

2. A problem well stated is half solved.—*How We Think.*

3. The way in which the problem is conceived decides what specific suggestions are entertained and which are dismissed; what data are selected and which rejected; it is the criterion for relevancy and irrelevancy of hypotheses and conceptual structures. On the other hand, to set up a problem that does not grow out of an actual situation is to start on a course of dead work.—*Logic: the Theory of Inquiry.*

See also: Culture 4; Hypotheses 3; Ideas 1; Interaction 2; Philosophers 3; Philosophy 3, 6; Science 9; Scientific Method 3.

PROCESS

Natural science is forced by its own development to abandon the assumption of fixity and to recognize that what for it is actually "universal" is *process*; but this fact of recent science still remains in philosophy, as in popular opinion up to the present time, a technical matter rather than what it is: namely, the most revolutionary discovery yet made.—Introduction to the 1948 edition of *Reconstruction in Philosophy.*

See also: Environment 5; Mind 5; Perfection.

PRODUCTION AND CONSUMPTION

1. The moment production is severed from immediate satisfaction, it becomes "labor."—*Human Nature and Conduct.*

2. The whole tendency of modern economic life has been to assume that consumption will take care of itself provided only production is grossly and intensely attended to. Making things is frantically accelerated; and every mechanical device is used to swell the senseless bulk. As a result most workers find no replenishment, no renewal and growth of mind, no fulfillment in work. They labor to get more means of later satisfaction. This procured is isolated in turn from production and is reduced to a barren physical affair or a sensuous compensation for normal goods denied. . . Production apart from fulfillment becomes purely a matter of quantity; for distinction, quality, is a matter of present meaning. Esthetic elements being excluded, the mechanical reign. Production lacks criteria; one thing is better than another if it can be made faster or in greater mass. Leisure is not the nourishment of mind in work, nor a recreation; it is a feverish hurry for diversion, excitement, display, otherwise there is no leisure except a sodden torpor. Fatigue due for some to monotony and for others to overstrain in maintaining the pace is inevitable.—*Ibid.*

PROGRESS

1. The good man not only measures his acts by a standard but he is concerned to revise his standard. The highest form of conscientiousness is interest in constant progress.—*Ethics* (with J. H. Tufts).

2. Progress is present reconstruction adding fullness and distinctness of meaning, and retrogression is a present slipping away of significance, determination, grasp. Those who hold that progress can be perceived and measured only by reference to a remote goal, first confuse meaning with space, and then treat spatial position as absolute, as limiting movement instead of being bounded in and by movement. . . Unless progress is a present reconstruction, it is nothing; if it cannot be told by

qualities belonging to the movement of transition it can never be judged.—*Human Nature and Conduct.*

3. Progress in civilization has not only meant increase in the scope and intricacy of problems to be dealt with, but it entails instability. For in multiplying wants, instruments and possibilities, it increases the variety of forces which enter into relations with one another and which have to be intelligently directed. . . From the standpoint of definite approximation to an ultimate goal, the balance falls heavily on the side of pessimism. The more striving, the more attainments, perhaps; but also assuredly the more needs and the more disappointments. The more we do and the more we accomplish, the more the end is vanity and vexation. From the standpoint of attainment of good that stays put, that constitutes a definite sum performed which lessens the amount of effort required in order to reach the ultimate goal of final good, progress is an illusion. But we are looking for it in the wrong place. The world war is a bitter commentary on the nineteenth century misconception of moral achievement—a misconception however which is only inherited from the traditional theory of fixed ends, attempting to bolster up that doctrine with aid from the "scientific" theory of evolution. The doctrine of progress is not yet bankrupt. The bankruptcy of the notion of fixed goods to be attained and stably possessed may possibly be the means of turning the mind of man to a tenable theory of progress—to attention to present troubles and possibilities.—*Ibid.*

See also: Education 3; Freedom 5; Loyalty 1; Youth 1.

PSYCHOLOGY

1. Psychology is the attempt to state in detail the machinery of the individual considered as the instrument and organ through which social action operates.—*The Influence of Darwin on Philosophy and Other Essays.*

2. Popular psychology is a mass of cant, of slush, and of superstition worthy of the most flourishing days of the medicine man.—*The Public and Its Problems.*

See also: Equality; Habit 6; Knowledge 1; Self 1.

PUBLIC OPINION

We are beginning to realize that emotions and imagination are more potent in shaping public sentiment and opinion than information and reason.—*Freedom and Culture.*

See also: Process.

R

READING

That a person can learn efficiently to read and yet not form a taste for reading good literature, or without having curiosities aroused that will lead him to apply his ability to read to explore fields outside of what is conventionally termed good reading matter, are sad facts of experience. Learning to read may develop book-worms, children who read omnivorously, but at the expense of development of social and executive abilities and skills. The question of what one learns to read is thus inextricably bound up with the question of *how* one learns to read. Unfortunately, experience shows that the methods which most readily and efficiently bring about skills to read (or write, or figure) in its narrower sense of ability to recognize, pronounce and put together words, do not at the same time take care of the formation of attitudes that decide the uses to which the ability is to be put.—*The Sources of a Science of Education.*

REALITY

1. Non-empirical realities are nonentities.—*The Influence of Darwin on Philosophy and Other Essays.*

2. Reality is a denotative term, a word used to designate indifferently everything that happens. Lies, dreams, insanities, deceptions, myths, theories are all of them just the events they

specifically are. Pragmatism is content to take its stand with science; for science finds all such events to be subject-matter of description and inquiry—just like stars and fossils, mosquitoes and malaria, circulation and vision.—In the *Creative Intelligence*: Essays in the Pragmatic Attitude (a Symposium).

3. Time and memory are true artists; they remold reality nearer to the heart's desire.—*Reconstruction in Philosophy*.

4. The method we term "scientific" forms for the modern man . . . the sole dependable means for disclosing the realities of existence.—"Credo," in *Living Philosophies* (a Symposium).
See also: Definition 2; Objects 2; Philosophy 5.

REASON

1. Reason is experimental intelligence.—*Reconstruction in Philosophy*.

2. Neither the existence nor the positive value of the irrational in man is to be glossed over. All the instincts, impulses, and emotions which push man into action outside the treadmill of use and wont are irrational. The depths, the mysteries of nature are non-rational. The business of reason is not to extinguish the fires which keep the cauldron of vitality seething, nor yet to supply the ingredients which are in vital stir. Its task is to see that they boil to some purpose.—*Characters and Events*.

3. Reasoning, as such, can provide means for effecting the change of conditions but by itself cannot effect it. Only execution of existential operations directed by an idea in which ratiocination terminates can bring about the rendering of environing conditions required to produce a settled and unified situation.—*Logic: the Theory of Inquiry*.
See also: Experience 5; Habit 1; Public Opinion.

RELATION

1. The distinguishing contribution of man is consciousness of the relations found in nature.—*Art as Experience*.

2. "Relation" is an ambiguous word. In philosophical discourse it is used to designate a connection instituted in thought. It then signifies something indirect, something purely intellectual, even logical. But "relation" in its idiomatic usage denotes something direct and active, something dynamic and energetic. It fixes attention upon the way things bear upon one another, their clashes and unitings, the way they fulfill and frustrate, promote and retard, excite and inhibit one another.—*Ibid.*

See also: International Relations; Law 2; Law of Nature 4; Thinking 11.

RELIGION

1. That science has the same spiritual import as supernaturalism; that democracy translates into the same religious attitude as did feudalism; that it is only a matter of slight changes in phraseology, a development of old symbolism into new shades of meaning—such beliefs testify to that torpor of imagination which is the uniform effect of dogmatic belief.—"Religion in Our Schools," in the *Hibbert Journal*, VI (1908).

2. Religion has been distorted into a possession—or burden —of a limited part of human nature, of a limited portion of humanity which finds no way to universalize religion except by imposing its own dogmas and ceremonies upon others.— *Human Nature and Conduct.*

3. Nowhere in the world at any time has religion been so thoroughly respectable as with us, and so nearly totally disconnected from life.—*Individualism, Old and New.*

4. A religion that began as a demand for a revolutionary change and that has become a sanction to established economic, political, and international institutions should perhaps lead its sincere devotees to reflect upon the sayings of the one worshipped as its founder: "Woe unto you when all men shall

speak well of you," and, "Blessed are ye when men shall revile you and persecute you."—"Credo," in *Living Philosophies* (a Symposium).

5. It seems to me that the chief danger to religion lies in the fact that it has become so respectable. It has become largely a sanction of what socially exists—a kind of gloss upon institutions and conventions.—*Ibid.*

6. Concretely there is no such thing as religion in the singular. There is only a multitude of religions.—*A Common Faith.*

7. A religion always signifies a special body of beliefs and practices having some kind of institutional organization, loose or tight. In contrast, the adjective "religious" denotes nothing in the way of a specifiable entity, either institutional or as a system of beliefs.—*Ibid.*

8. Any activity pursued in behalf of an ideal and against obstacles and in spite of threats of personal loss because of conviction of its general and enduring value is religious in quality.—*Ibid.*

9. It is sometimes held that beliefs about religious matters are symbolic, like rites and ceremonies. This view may be an advance upon that which holds to their literal objective validity. But as usually put forward it suffers from an ambiguity. Of what are the beliefs symbols? Are they symbols of things experienced in other modes than those set apart as religious, so that the things symbolized have an independent standing? Or are they symbols in the sense of standing for some transcendental reality—transcendental because not being the subject-matter of experience generally? Even the fundamentalist admits a certain quality and degree of symbolism in the latter sense in objects of religious belief. For he holds that the objects of these beliefs are so far beyond finite human capacity that our beliefs must be couched in more or less metaphorical terms. The conception that faith is the best available substitute for knowledge

113

in our present estate still attaches to the notion of the symbolic character of the materials of faith; unless by ascribing to them a symbolic nature we mean that these materials stand for something that is verifiable in general and public experience.

Were we to adopt the latter point of view, it would be evident not only that the intellectual articles of a creed must be understood to be symbolic of moral and other ideal values, but that the facts taken to be historic and used as concrete evidence of the intellectual articles are themselves symbolic. These articles of a creed present events and persons that have been made over by the idealistic imagination in the interest, at their best, of moral ideals. . . It is admitted that the objects of religion are ideal in contrast with our present state. What would be lost if it were also admitted that they have authoritative claim upon conduct just because they are ideal? The assumption that these objects of religion exist already in some realm of Being seems to add nothing to their force, while it weakens their claim over us as ideals, in so far as it bases that claim upon matters that are intellectually dubious. The question narrows itself to this: Are the ideals that move us genuinely ideal or are they ideal only in contrast with our present estate?—*A Common Faith.*
See also: Authority 4; Mind 1; School 7.

RESPONSIBILITY

1. By responsibility as an element in intellectual attitude is meant the disposition to consider in advance the probable consequences of any projected step and deliberately to accept them: to accept them in the sense of taking them into account, acknowledging them in action, not yielding a mere verbal assent.—*Democracy and Education.*

2. Liability is the beginning of responsibility. We are held accountable by others for the consequences of our acts. They visit their like and dislike of these consequences upon us. In

vain do we claim that these are not ours; that they are products of ignorance not design, or are incidents in the execution of a most laudable scheme. Their authorship is imputed to us. We are disapproved, and disapproval is not an inner state of mind but a most definite act. Others say to us by their deeds we do not care a fig whether you did this deliberately or not. . . The reference in blame and every unfavorable judgment is prospective, not retrospective. Theories about responsibility may become confused, but in practice no one is stupid enough to try to change the past. Approbation and disapprobation are ways of influencing the formation of habits and aims; that is, of influencing future acts. The individual is held accountable for what he has done in order that he may be responsive in what he is going to do.—*Human Nature and Conduct.*

3. There can be no stable and balanced development of mind and character apart from the assumption of responsibility.—*Individualism, Old and New.*

4. Ours is the responsibility of conserving, transmitting, rectifying, and expanding the heritage of values we have received that those who come after us may receive it more solid and more secure, more widely accessible and more generously shared than we have received it.—*A Common Faith.*

5. Incapacity to assume responsibilities involved in having a voice in shaping policies is bred and increased by conditions in which that responsibility is denied.—"Democracy and Educational Administration," in *School and Society,* XLV (1937).

See also: Democracy 2; Freedom 6; Human Concerns; Individuality 2; Intelligence 1; School 2.

REVOLUTION

The cost of revolutions must be charged up to those who have taken for their aim arrest of custom instead of its readjustment.—*Human Nature and Conduct.*

See also: Conservatism 2; Religion 4.

RIGHT

1. Right is only an abstract name for the multitude of concrete demands in action which others impress upon us, and of which we are obliged, if we would live, to take some account. Its authority is the exigency of their demands, the efficacy of their insistencies. There may be good ground for the contention that in theory the idea of the right is subordinate to that of the good, being a statement of the course proper to attain good. But in fact it signifies the totality of social pressures exercised upon us to induce us to think and desire in certain ways. Hence the right can in fact become the road to the good only as the elements that compose this unremitting pressure are enlightened, only as social relationships become themselves reasonable. —*Human Nature and Conduct.*

2. The concept of Rightness, in many cases, is independent of the concept of satisfaction and good. When a parent says "this is right and therefore you should do it," it is to be hoped that the performance of the act will actually conduce to some good. But as an idea, "right" introduces an element which is quite outside that of the good. This element is that of exaction, demand. . . Citizens in a just state respond at their personal inconvenience to the demands of the state, not because the latter may bring physical pressure or mental coercion to bear upon them, but because they are members of organized society: members in such an intimate sense that the demands are not external impositions even when they run counter to the good which a present desire calls for. The claims of friendship are not always agreeable; sometimes they may be extremely irksome. But we should not hesitate to say that one who refused to meet them merely because they were troublesome was no true friend. If we generalize such instances, we reach the conclusion that Right, law, duty, arise from the relations which human beings intimately sustain to one another, and that their authoritative force springs from the very nature of the relation

that binds people together.—*Ethics* (with J. H. Tufts; revised ed.).

3. Natural rights and natural liberties exist only in the kingdom of mythological social zoology.—*Liberalism and Social Action.*

See also: Equality; Freedom 10; Selfishness.

S

SCHOOL

1. Some few years ago I was looking about the school supply stores in the city, trying to find desks and chairs which seemed thoroughly suitable from all points of view—artistic, hygienic, and educational—to the needs of children. We had a great deal of difficulty in finding what we needed, and finally one dealer, more intelligent than the rest, made this remark: "I am afraid we have not what you want. You want something at which the children may work; these are all for listening."

That tells the story of traditional education. It is all made "for listening"—because simply studying lessons out of a book is only another kind of listening; it marks the dependency of one mind upon another. The attitude of listening means comparatively speaking, passivity, absorption; that there are certain ready-made materials which are there, which have been prepared by the school superintendent, the board, the teacher, and of which the child is to take in as much as possible in the least possible time.

There is very little place in the traditional schoolroom for the child to work. The workshop, the laboratory, the materials, the tools with which the child may construct, create, and actively inquire, and even the requisite space, have been for the most part lacking. The things that have to do with these processes

have not even a definitely recognized place in education.—
School and Society.

2. I find the fundamental need of the school today dependent
upon its limited recognition of the principle of freedom of intelligence. This limitation appears to me to affect both of the
elements of school life: teacher and pupil. As to both, the school
has lagged behind the general contemporary social movement;
and much that is unsatisfactory, much of conflict and of defeat,
comes from the discrepancy between the relatively undemo-
cratic organization of the school, as it affects the mind of both
teacher and pupil, and the growth and extension of the democratic principle in life beyond school doors. . .

Until the public-school system is organized in such a way that
every teacher has some regular and representative way in which
he or she can register judgment upon matters of educational
importance, with the assurance that this judgment will somehow affect the school system, the assertion that the present system is not, from the internal standpoint, democratic seems to
be justified. Either we come here upon some fixed and inherent
limitation of the democratic principle, or else we find in this
fact an obvious discrepancy between the conduct of the schools
and the conduct of social life—a discrepancy so great as to
demand immediate and persistent effort at reform. . .

I know it will be said that this state of things, while an evil,
is a necessary one; that without it confusion and chaos would
reign; that such regulations are the inevitable accompaniments
of any graded system. It is said that the average teacher is in-
competent to take any part in laying out the course of study or
in initiating methods of instruction or discipline. Is not this the
type of argument which has been used from time immemorial
and in every department of life, against the advance of democracy? What does democracy mean save that the individual
is to have a share in determining the conditions and the aims of
his own work; and that upon the whole, through the free and

mutual harmonizing of different individuals, the work of the world is better done than when planned, arranged, and directed by a few, no matter how wise or of how good intent that few? How can we justify our belief in the democratic principle elsewhere, and then go back entirely upon it when we come to education?

Moreover, the argument proves too much. The more it is asserted that the existing corps of teachers is unfit to have voice in the settlement of important educational matters, and their unfitness to exercise intellectual initiative and to assume the responsibility for constructive work is emphasized, the more their unfitness to attempt the much more difficult and delicate task of guiding souls appears. If this body is so unfit, how can it be trusted to carry out the recommendations of the dictations of the wisest body of experts? If teachers are incapable of the intellectual responsibility which goes with the determination of the methods they are to use in teaching, how can they employ methods when dictated by others, in other than a mechanical, capricious, and clumsy manner? The argument, I say, proves too much.

Moreover, if the teaching force is as inept and unintelligent and irresponsible as the argument assumes, surely the primary problem is that of their improvement. Only by sharing in some responsible task does there come a fitness to share in it. The argument that we must wait until men and women are fully ready to assume intellectual and social responsibilities would have defeated every step in the democratic direction that has ever been taken. The prevalence of methods of authority and of external dictation and direction tends automatically to perpetuate the very conditions of inefficiency, lack of interest, inability to assume positions of self-determination, which constitute the reasons that are depended upon to justify the regime of authority.—"Democracy in Education," in the *Elementary School Teacher*, IV (1903).

3. To an extent characteristic of no other institution, save that of the state itself, the school has power to modify the social order.—*Moral Principles in Education* (a Monograph, ed. by H. Suzallo).

4. What is learned in school is at the best only a small part of education, a relatively superficial part; and yet what is learned in school makes artificial distinctions in society and marks persons off from one another. Consequently we exaggerate school learning compared with what is gained in the ordinary course of living.—*Schools of To-Morrow* (with Evelyn Dewey).

5. We send children to school supposedly to learn in a systematic way the occupations which constitute living, but to a very large extent the schools overlook, in the methods and subject-matter of their teaching, the social basis of living. Instead of centering the work in the concrete, the human side of things, they put the emphasis on the abstract, hence the work is made academic—unsocial. Work then is no longer connected with a group of people all engaged in occupations, but is isolated, selfish and individualistic. It is based on a conception of society which no longer fits the facts.—*Ibid.*

6. Our schooling does not educate, if by education be meant a trained habit of discriminating inquiry and discriminating belief, the ability to look beneath a floating surface to detect the conditions that fix the contour of the surface, and the forces which create its waves and drifts. We dupe ourselves and others because we have not that inward protection against sensation, excitement, credulity, and conventionally stereotyped opinion which is found only in a trained mind.

This fact determines the fundamental criticism to be leveled against current schooling, against what passes as an educational system. It not only does little to make discriminating intelligence a safeguard against surrender to the invasion of bunk —but it does much to favor susceptibility to a welcoming reception of it. There appear to be two chief causes for this ineptitude. One is the persistence, in the body of what is taught, of traditional material which is irrelevant to present conditions —subject-matter of instruction which though valuable in some past period is so remote from the perplexities and issues of present life that its mastery, even if fairly adequate, affords no resource for discriminating insight, no protection against being duped in facing the emergencies of today. From the standpoint of this criterion of education, a large portion of current material of instruction is simply aside from the mark. . .

The other way in which schooling fosters an indiscriminating gulping mental habit, eager to be duped, is positive. It consists in a systematic, almost deliberate, avoidance of the spirit of criticism in dealing with history, politics, and economics. There is an implicit belief that this avoidance is the only way by which to produce good citizens. The more undiscriminatingly the history and institutions of one's own nation are idealized, the greater is the likelihood, so it is assumed, that the school product will be a loyal patriot, a well equipped good citizen. . .

The effect is to send students out into actual life in a condition of acquired and artificial innocence. Such perceptions as they may have of the realities of social struggles and problems they have derived accidentally, by the way, and without the safeguards of intelligent acquaintance with facts and impartially conducted discussion. It is no wonder that they are ripe to be gulled, or that their attitude is one which merely perpetuates existing confusion, ignorance, prejudice, and credulity. . .

What will happen if teachers become sufficiently courageous and emancipated to insist that education means the creation of a discriminating mind, a mind that prefers not to dupe itself or to be the dupe of others? Clearly they will have to cultivate the habit of suspended judgment, of skepticism, of desire for evidence, of appeal to observation rather than sentiment, discussion rather than bias, inquiry rather than conventional idealizations. When this happens schools will be the dangerous outposts of a humane civilization. But they will also begin to be supremely interesting places.—*Characters and Events*, II.

7. Just as schools have been led by actual conditions to be non-sectarian in religion, and thus have been forced to evade important questions about the bearings of contemporary science and historical knowledge upon traditional religious beliefs, so they have tended to become colorless, because neutral, in most of the vital social issues of the day. The practical result is an indiscriminate complacency about actual conditions. The evil goes much deeper than the production of a split between theory and practice and the creating of a corresponding unreality in theory. Our educational undertakings are left without unified direction and without the ardor and enthusiasm that are generated when educational activities are organically connected with dominant social purpose and conviction. Lacking direction by definite social ideals, these undertakings become the victims of special pressure groups, the subjects of contending special interests, the sport of passing intellectual fashions, the toys of dominant personalities who impress for a time their special opinions, the passive tools of antiquated traditions. They supply students with technical instrumentalities for realizing such purposes as outside conditions breed in them. They accomplish little in forming the basic desires and purposes which determine special activities.—In *The Educational Frontier* (a Symposium, ed. by W. H. Kilpatrick).

8. Even in the classroom we are beginning to learn that learning that develops intelligence and character does not come about when only the textbook and the teacher have a say, that every individual becomes educated only as he has an opportunity to contribute something from his own experience, no matter how meager or slender that background of experience may be at a given time, and finally that enlightenment comes

from the give and take, from the exchange of experience and ideas. The realization of that principle in the schoolroom, it seems to me, is an expression of the significance of democracy as an educational process without which individuals cannot come either into the full possession of themselves or make a contribution, if they have it in them to make, to the social well-being of others, to the welfare of the whole of which they are a part.—*Problems of Men.*

9. All institutions are educational in the sense that they operate to form the attitudes, dispositions, abilities and disabilities that constitute a concrete personality. The principle applies with special force to the school. For it is the main business of the family and the school to influence directly the formation and growth of attitudes and dispositions, emotional, intellectual and moral. Whether this educative process is carried on in a predominantly democratic or non-democratic way becomes, therefore, a question of transcendent importance not only for education itself but for the final effect upon all the interests and activities of a society that is committed to the democratic way of life. Hence, if the general tenor of what I have said about the democratic ideal and method is anywhere near the truth, it must be said that the democratic principle requires that every teacher should have some regular and organic way in which he can, directly or through representatives democratically chosen, participate in the formation of the controlling aims, methods and materials of the school of which he is a part.—*Ibid.*

See also: Community 2; Discipline 1; Education 4, 12; Freedom 5; Growth 2; Judgment 2; Knowledge 2; Learning 1, 2; Theory 2.

SCIENCE

1. It is only the worn-out cynic, the devitalized sensualist, and the fanatical dogmatist who interpret the continuous change

of science as proving that, since each successive statement is wrong, the whole record is error and folly and that the present truth is only the error not yet found out.—*Essays in Experimental Logic.*

2. Science has led men to look to the future instead of the past.—*Democracy and Education.*

3. Every great advance in science has issued from a new audacity of imagination.—*The Quest for Certainty.*

4. Science signifies, I take it, the existence of systematic methods of inquiry, which, when they are brought to bear on a range of facts, enable us to understand them better and to control them more intelligently, less haphazardly and with less routine.—*Sources of a Science of Education.*

5. If there were an opposition between science and art, I should be compelled to side with those who assert that education is an art. But there is no opposition, although there is a distinction. We must not be misled by words. Engineering is, in actual practice, an art. But it is an art that progressively incorporates more and more of science into itself, more of mathematics, physics and chemistry. It is the kind of art it is precisely because of a content of scientific subject-matter which guides it as a practical operation. There is room for the original and daring projects of exceptional individuals. But their distinction lies not in the fact that they turn their backs upon science, but in the fact that they make new integrations of scientific material and turn it to new and previously unfamiliar and unforeseen uses.—*Ibid.*

6. Because science starts with questions and inquiries it is fatal to all social system-making and programs of fixed ends. —*Individualism, Old and New.*

7. As long as we worship science and are afraid of philosophy we shall have no great science.—*Philosophy and Civilization.*

8. Science is not constituted by any particular body of sub-

ject-matter. It is constituted by a method, a method of changing beliefs by means of tested inquiry.—*A Common Faith.*

9. The scientific attitude . . . is rooted in the problems that are set and questions that are raised by the conditions of actuality. The unscientific attitude is that which shuns such problems, which runs away from them, or covers them up instead of facing them. . . Positively, it is the will to inquire, to examine, to discriminate, to draw conclusions only on the basis of evidence after taking pains to gather all available evidence. —"Unity of Science as a Social Problem," in the *International Encyclopedia of Unified Science,* Vol. I, No. 1 (1938).

See also: Abstraction 2; Authority 4; Hypotheses 3; Knowledge 1, 9; Law of Nature 3; Logic 1; Matter 2, 3; Philosophy 7; Process; Reality 2; Religion 1; Society 5; Value 1; World 2.

SCIENTIFIC METHOD

1. We use scientific method in directing physical but not human energies.—*Individualism, Old and New.*

2. Scientific method . . . is but systematic, extensive, and carefully controlled use of alert and unprejudiced observation and experimentation in collecting, arranging, and testing evidence.—"Antinaturalism in Extremis," in *Naturalism and the Human Spirit* (a Symposium, ed. by Y. H. Krikorian).

3. Since scientific methods simply exhibit free intelligence operating in the best manner available at a given time, the cultural waste, confusion, and distortion that result from the failure to use these methods, in all fields in connection with all problems, is incalculable.—*Logic: the Theory of Inquiry.*

4. Insistence upon numerical measurement, when it is not inherently required by the consequence to be effected, is a mark of respect for the ritual of scientific practice at the expense of its substance.—*Ibid.*

See also: Authority 4; Experimental Method; Objects 2; Reality 4; Tolerance 3.

SECURITY

1. Man who lives in a world of hazards is compelled to seek security. He has sought to attain it in two ways. One of them began with an attempt to propitiate the powers which environ him and determine his destiny. It expressed itself in supplication, sacrifice, ceremonial rite and magical cult. In time these crude methods were largely displaced. The sacrifice of a contrite heart was esteemed more pleasing than that of bulls and oxen; the inner attitude of reverence and devotion more desirable than external ceremonies. If man could not conquer destiny he could willingly ally himself with it; putting his will, even in sore affliction, on the side of the powers which dispense fortune, he could escape defeat and might triumph in the midst of destruction.

The other course is to invent arts and by their means turn the powers of nature to account; man constructs a fortress out of the very conditions and forces which threaten him. He builds shelters, weaves garments, makes flame his friend instead of his enemy, and grows into the complicated arts of associated living. This is the method of changing the world through action, as the other is the method of changing the self in emotion and idea. It is a commentary on the slight control man has obtained over himself by means of control over nature, that the method of action has been felt to manifest dangerous pride, even defiance of the powers which be.—*The Quest for Certainty.*

2. Any system that cannot provide elementary security for millions has no claim to the title of being organized in behalf of liberty and the development of individuals. Any person and any movement whose interest in these ends is genuine and not a cover for personal advantage and power must put primary

emphasis in thought and action upon the means of their attainment.—*Problems of Men.*

See also: Freedom 6; Interaction 4.

SELF

1. We find the unity of the psychical processes . . . and therefore their ultimate explanation, in the fact that man is a self.—*Psychology.*
2. The self reveals its nature by what it chooses.—*Ethics* (with J. H. Tufts).
3. The self is not something ready-made, but something in continuous formation through choice of action.—*Democracy and Education.*
4. When dominating religious ideas were built up about the idea that the self is a stranger and pilgrim in this world; when morals, falling in line, found true good only in inner states of a self accessible to anything but its own private introspection; when political theory assumed the finality of disconnected and mutually exclusive personalities, the notion that the bearer of experience is antithetical to the world instead of being in and of it was congenial. It at least had the warrant of other beliefs and aspirations. But the doctrine of biological continuity of organic evolution has destroyed the scientific basis of the conception...

If biological development be accepted, the subject of experience is at least an animal, continuous with other organic forms in a process of more complex organization. An animal in turn is at least continuous with chemico-physical processes which, in living things, are so organized as really to constitute the activities of life with all their defining traits. And experience is not identical with brain action; it is the entire organic agent-patient in all its interaction with the environment, natural and social.—In the *Creative Intelligence*: Essays in the Pragmatic Attitude (a Symposium).

5. We can't help being individual selves, each one of us. If selfhood as such is a bad thing, the blame lies not with the self but with the universe, with providence. But in fact the distinction between a selfishness with which we find fault and an unselfishness which we esteem is found in the quality of the activities which we proceed from and enter into the self, according as they are contractive, exclusive, or expansive, outreaching. Meaning exists for some self, but this truistic fact doesn't fix the quality of any particular meaning. It may be such as to make the self small, or such as to exalt and dignify the self. It is as impertinent to decry the worth of experience because it is connected with a self as it is fantastic to idealize personality just as personality aside from the question what sort of a person one is.—*Human Nature and Conduct.*

6. The organism—the self, the subject of action—is a factor within experience and not something outside of it to which experiences are attached as the self's private property. According to my view a characterization of any aspect, phase, or element of experience as *mine* is not a description of its direct experience but a description of experience with respect to some special problem for some special purpose, one which needs to be specified.—Reply in *The Philosophy of John Dewey* (a Symposium, ed. by. P. A. Schilpp).

See also: Experience 7; Knowledge 1; Selfishness; Universe 2; Words 4.

SELFISHNESS

Acts are not selfish because they evince consideration for the future well-being of the self. No one would say that deliberate care for one's own health, sufficiency, progress in learning is bad just because it is one's own. It is moral duty upon occasion to look out for oneself in these respects. Such acts acquire the quality of moral selfishness only when they are indulged in so as to manifest obtuseness to the claims of others. An act is not wrong because it advances the well-being of the self, but because it is unfair, inconsiderate, in respect to the rights, just claims, of others.—*Ethics* (with J. H. Tufts; revised ed.).

See also: Children 1; Human Nature 4; Peace; School 5; Self 5.

SKEPTICISM

Skepticism that is not . . . a search is as much a personal indulgence as is dogmatism.—*The Quest for Certainty.*

See also: School 6.

SOCIAL PSYCHOLOGY

The problem of social psychology is not how either individual or collective mind forms social groups and customs, but how different customs, established interacting arrangements, form and nurture different minds.—*Human Nature and Conduct.*

SOCIETY

1. What nutrition and reproduction are to physiological life, education is to social life.—*Democracy and Education.*

2. Society is one word, but infinitely many things. It covers all the ways in which by associating together men share their experiences, and build up common interests and aims.—*Reconstruction in Philosophy.*

3. Society is the process of associating in such ways that experience, ideas, emotions, values are transmitted and made common.—*Ibid.*

4. "Society" is either an abstract or a collective noun. In the concrete, there are societies, associations, groups of an immense number of kinds, having ties and instituting different interests. They may be gangs, criminal bands; clubs for sport,

sociability, and eating; scientific and professional organizations; political parties and unions within them; families; religious denominations, business partnerships, and corporations; and so on in an endless list. The associations may be local, nation-wide, and trans-national. Since there is no one thing which may be called society, except their indefinite overlappings, there is no unqualified eulogistic connotation adhering to the term "society." Some societies are in the main to be approved; some to be condemned, on account of their consequences upon the character and conduct of those engaged in them and because of their remoter consequences upon others. All of them, like all things human, are mixed in quality; "society" is something to be approved and judged critically and discriminatingly. "Socialization" of some sort—that is, the reflex modification of wants, beliefs, and work because of share in a united action—is inevitable. But it is as marked in the formation of frivolous, dissipated, fanatical, narrow-minded, and criminal persons as in that of competent inquirers, learned scholars, creative artists, and good neighbors.—*The Public and Its Problems.*

5. Society, in order to solve its own problems and remedy its own ills, needs to employ science and technology for social instead of merely private ends. This need for a society in which experimental inquiry and planning for social ends are organically contained is also the need for a new education.—*The Educational Frontier* (a Symposium, ed. by. W. H. Kilpatrick).

See also: Democracy 3; Education 9; Individual 3; Interaction 2, 3; Liberty 1; Right 2; School 4, 5.

SOUL

Some bodies have soul as some conspicuously have fragrance. To make this statement is to call attention to properties that characterize these bodies, not to import a mysterious non-natural entity or force. . . . But the idiomatic non-doctrinal use of the word "soul" retains a sense of the realities concerned. To say emphatically of a particular person that he has soul or a great soul is not to utter a platitude, applicable generally to all human beings. It expresses the conviction that the man or woman in question has in marked degrees qualities of sensitive, rich and coordinated participation in all the situations of life. Thus works of art, music, poetry, painting, architecture have soul, while others are dead, mechanical.—*Experience and Nature.*

See also: Words 4.

SPEECH

1. Speech forms are our great carriers; the easy-running vehicles by which meanings are transported from experiences that no longer concern us to those that are as yet dark and dubious.—*How We Think.*

2. Language exists only when it is listened to as well as spoken. The hearer is an indispensable partner. . . . There is the speaker, the thing said, and the one spoken to.—*Experience and Nature.*

See also: Language.

STATE

1. To explain the origin of the state by saying that man is a political animal is to travel in a verbal circle.—*The Public and Its Problems.*

2. The state is the organization of the public effected through officials for the protection of the interests shared by its members. —*Ibid.*

3. The state is as its officers are.—*Ibid.*

4. We tend to submit individuality to the state instead of acting upon the belief that the state in its constitution, laws, and

administration, can be made the means of furthering the ends of a community of free individuals.—*Problems of Men.*

See also: Right 2; School 3.

STIMULUS AND RESPONSE

1. The distinction of sensation and movement as stimulus and response respectively is not a distinction which can be regarded as descriptive of anything which holds of psychical events.—"The Reflex Arc Concept in Psychology," in the *Psychological Review*, III (1896).

2. Every stimulus directs activity. It does not simply excite it or stir it up, but directs it toward an object. Put the other way around, a response is not just a reaction, a protest, as it were, against being disturbed; it is, as the word indicates, an answer. It meets the stimulus, and corresponds with it. There is an adaptation of the stimulus and response to each other. A light is the stimulus to the eye to see something, and the business of the eye is to see. If the eyes are open and there is light, seeing occurs; the stimulus is but a condition of the fulfillment of the proper function of the organ, not an outside interruption.— *Democracy and Education.*

See also: Democracy 3; Habit 1, 6.

SYMBOLS

1. Symbols . . . are condensed substitutes of actual things and events.—*Experience and Nature.*

2. The invention or discovery of symbols is doubtless by far the single greatest event in the history of man. Without them, no intellectual advance is possible; with them, there is no limit set to intellectual development except inherent stupidity.—*The Quest for Certainty.*

See also: Language 2; Mathematics 2, 3; Mind 2; Religion 1, 9.

T

TEACHING

1. It is the teacher's business to know what powers are striving for utterance at a given period in the child's development, and what sorts of activity will bring these to helpful expression, in order then to supply the requisite stimuli and needed materials.—In the *Elementary School Record* (Monograph I, 1900).

2. Utilizing of interest and habit to make of it something fuller, wider, something more refined and under better control, might be defined as the teacher's whole duty.—*Educational Essays* (ed. by J. J. Findlay).

3. The educator's part in the enterprise of education is to furnish the environment which stimulates responses and directs the learner's course.—*Democracy and Education*.

4. Teaching may be compared to selling commodities. No one can sell unless someone buys. We should ridicule a merchant who said that he had sold a great many goods although no one had bought any. But perhaps there are teachers who think that they have done a good day's teaching irrespective of what pupils have learned. . . . The only way to increase the learning of pupils is to augment the quantity and quality of real learning. Since learning is something that the pupil has to do himself and for himself, the initiative lies with the learner. The

teacher is a guide and director; he steers the boat, but the energy that propels it must come from those who are learning. The more a teacher is aware of the past experiences of students, of their hopes, desires, chief interests, the better will he understand the forces at work that need to be directed and utilized for the formation of reflective habits.—*How We Think*.

5. Teachers . . . being human, may substitute dogmas for hypotheses, mistake propaganda for teaching, novelty for depth, and the very subjects that most need free inquiry and that may most readily excite intellectual interest in young people become subject to a kind of perversion, influential in the measure of its vague intangibility.—*Education Today* (ed. by J. Ratner).

6. We talk about democracy in the classroom but give it nothing but lip-service. Oftentimes our schools impose uniformity as well as conformity upon both teachers and children. . . . Unless the teacher is permitted to retain all the rights and privileges of any other citizen, teaching will become a social stigma instead of an honor.—From an *Interview* by Benjamin Fine in October, 1949.

See also: Discipline 1; Learning 2; School 2, 9.

THEORY

1. There is no inherent opposition between theory and practice; the former enlarges, releases and gives significance to the latter; while practice supplies theory with its materials and with the test and check which keep it sincere and vital.—"Individuality and Experience," in the *Journal of the Barnes Foundation*, II (1926).

2. Theory is in the end, as has been well said, the most practical of all things, because this widening of the range of attention beyond nearby purpose and desire eventually results in the creation of wider and further-reaching purposes and enables us to use a much wider and deeper range of conditions

and means than were expressed in the observation of primitive practical purposes. For the time being, however, the formation of theories demands a resolute turning aside from the needs of practical operations previously performed.

This detachment is peculiarly hard to secure in the case of those persons who are concerned with building up the scientific content of educational practices and arts. There is a pressure for immediate results, for a demonstration of a quick, short span of usefulness in school. There is a tendency to convert the results of statistical inquiries and laboratory experiments into directions and rules for the conduct of school administration and instruction. Results tend to be directly grabbed, as it were, and put into operation by teachers. Then there is not the leisure for that slow gradual independent growth of theories that is the necessary condition of the formation of a true science.—*Sources of a Science of Education.*

3. Theory separated from concrete doing and making is empty and futile. . . . The problem of the relation of theory and practice is not a problem of theory alone; it is that, but it is also the most practical problem of life. For it is the question of how intelligence may inform action, and how action may bear the fruit of increased insight into meaning.—*The Quest for Certainty.*

4. Theories as they are used in scientific inquiry are themselves matters of systematic abstraction. Like ideas, they get away from what may be called the immediately given facts in order to be applicable to a much fuller range of relevant facts. —*Knowing and the Known.*

See also: Abstraction 3; Experimental Method 4; Hypotheses 3; Objects 2; Philosophy 2.

THINKING

1. Thought deals not with bare things, but with their meanings.—*How We Think.*

2. A being who could not think without training could never be trained to think; one may have to learn to think well, but not to think.—*Ibid.*

3. Active, persistent, and careful consideration of any belief or supposed form of knowledge in the light of the grounds that support it, and the further conclusions to which it tends, constitutes reflective thought.—*Ibid.*

4. Thinking begins in what may fairly enough be called a forked road situation, a situation which is ambiguous, which presents a dilemma, which proposes alternatives.—*How We Think.*

5. The function of reflective thought is to transform a situation in which there is experienced obscurity, doubt, conflict, disturbance of some sort, into a situation that is clear, coherent, settled, harmonious.—*Ibid.*

6. The need of thinking to accomplish something beyond thinking is more potent than thinking for its own sake.—*Ibid.*

7. It does not pay to tether one's thoughts to the post of use with too short a rope.—*How We Think.*

8. The person who really thinks learns quite as much from his failures as from his successes.—*Ibid.*

9. Thinking . . . is far from being the armchair thing it is often supposed to be. The reason it is not an armchair thing is that it is not an event going on exclusively within the cortex, or the cortex and vocal organs. It involves the explorations by which relevant data are procured and the physical analyses by which they are refined and made precise; it comprises the readings by which information is got hold of, the words which are experimented with, and the calculations by which the significance of entertained conceptions or hypotheses is elaborated. Hands and feet, apparatus and appliances of all kinds are as much a part of it as changes in the brain.—*Essays in Experimental Logic.*

10. Thinking is the method of intelligent learning, of learn-

ing that employs and rewards minds.—*Democracy and Education.*

11. Thinking is equivalent to an explicit rendering of the intelligent element of our experience. It makes it possible to act with an end in view. It is the condition of our having aims. As soon as an infant begins to expect he begins to use something which is now going on as a sign of something to follow; he is, in however simple a fashion, judging. For he takes one thing as evidence of something else, and so recognizes a relationship. Any future development, however elaborate it may be, is only an extending and a refining of this simple act of inference. All that the wisest man can do is to observe what is going on more widely and more minutely, and then select more carefully from what is noted just those factors which point to something which is to happen. . . . To fill our heads, like a scrapbook, with this and that item as a finished and done-for thing, is not to think. It is to turn ourselves into a piece of registering apparatus. To consider the bearing of the occurrence upon what may be, but is not yet, is to think.—*Ibid.*

12. All serious thinking combines in some proportion and perspective the actual and the possible, where actuality supplies contact and solidity while possibility furnishes the ideal upon which criticism rests and from which creative effort springs.—*Characters and Events.*

13. We think in terms of classes, as we concretely experience in terms of individuals.—*Art as Experience.*

14. Reflection is an indirect response to the environment.—"The Development of American Pragmatism," in the *Twentieth Century Philosophy* (a Symposium, ed. by D. D. Runes).

See also: Conservatism 1; Habits 2, 3; Ideas 3; Words 1.

TOLERANCE

1. Almost all men have learned the lesson of tolerance with respect to past heresies and divisions.—*Characters and Events.*

2. Toleration is not just an attitude of good-humored indifference. It is positive willingness to permit reflection and inquiry to go on in the faith that the truly right will be rendered more secure through questioning and discussion, while things which have endured merely from custom will be amended or done away with. Toleration of difference in moral judgment is a duty which those most insistent upon duty find it hardest to learn.—*Ethics* (with J. H. Tufts, revised ed.).

3. Toleration of diverse views, freedom of communication, the distribution of what is found out to every individual as the ultimate intellectual consumer, are involved in the democratic as in the scientific method.—*Freedom and Culture.*

See also: Democracy 10; Understanding 2.

TRUTH

1. To select truth as objective and error as "subjective" is, on this basis, an unjustifiably partial procedure. . . . It is human to regard the course of events which is in line with our own efforts as the regular course of events, and interruptions as abnormal, but this partiality of human desire is itself a part of what actually takes place.—In the *Creative Intelligence:* Essays in the Pragmatic Attitude (a Symposium).

2. The true means the verified and means nothing else.— *Reconstruction in Philosophy.*

3. Truths are but one class of meanings, namely, those in which a claim to verifiability by their consequences is an intrinsic part of their meaning. Beyond this island of meanings which in their own nature are true or false lies the ocean of meanings to which truth and falsity are irrelevant. . . . We may indeed ask for the truth of Shakespeare's *Hamlet* or Shelley's *Skylark*, but by truth we now signify something quite different from that of scientific statement and historical record. —*Philosophy and Civilization.*

4. There is but one sure road of access to truth—the road of patient, cooperative inquiry operating by means of observation, equipment, record and controlled reflection.—*A Common Faith.*

See also: Experience 5; Freedom of Thought 2; Hypotheses 2; Morality 5; Science 1.

U

UNDERSTANDING

1. A being that cannot understand at all is at least protected from misunderstanding.—*How We Think.*

2. Every extension of intelligence as the method of action enlarges the area of common understanding. Understanding may not ensure complete agreement, but it gives the only sound basis for enduring agreement. In any case where there is a difference, it will conduce to agreement to differ, to mutual tolerance and sympathy, pending the time when more adequate knowledge and better methods of judging are at hand.—In *The Educational Frontier* (a Symposium, ed. by W. H. Kilpatrick).

3. What will it profit a man to do this, that, and the other specific thing, if he has no clear idea of why he is doing them? —*Education Today* (ed. by J. Ratner).

4. Understanding has to be in terms of how things work and how to do things. Understanding, by its very nature, is related to action; just as information, by its very nature, is isolated from action or connected with it only here and there by accident.— *Problems of Men.*

5. The Understanding is not free to judge in any arbitrary sense of freedom. To attain knowledge we must judge or under-

stand in necessary ways, or else we do not attain knowledge of objects but only personal fancies.—*Ibid.*

See also: Belief 4; Community 1; Man 2; Open-mindedness 3; Science 4.

UNIVERSE

1. To idealize and rationalize the universe at large is a confession of inability to master the courses of things that specifically concern us.—*The Influence of Darwin on Philosophy and Other Essays.*

2. The self is always directed toward something beyond itself and so its own unification depends upon the idea of the integration of the shifting scenes of the world into that imaginative totality we call the Universe.—*A Common Faith.*

3. The feature of unification is generalized beyond the limits in which it takes place, namely resolution of specific problematic situations; knowledge then is supposed to consist of attainment of a final all-comprehensive Unity, equivalent to the Universe as an unconditioned whole.—*Logic: the Theory of Inquiry.*

See also: Chance; Mind 4.

V

VALUE

1. Physical science has for the time being far outrun psychical. We have mastered the physical mechanism sufficiently to turn out possible goods; we have not gained a knowledge of the conditions through which possible values become actual in life, and so are still at the mercy of habit, of haphazard, and hence of force.—*The Influence of Darwin on Philosophy and Other Essays.*

2. The term "value" has two quite different meanings. On the one hand, it denotes the attitude of prizing a thing, finding it worth while, for its own sake or intrinsically. This is a name for a full or complete experience. To value in this sense is to appreciate. But to value also means a distinctly intellectual act —an operation of comparing and judging—to evaluate. This occurs when direct full experience is lacking, and the question arises which of the various possibilities of a situation is to be preferred in order to reach a full realization, or vital experience.—*Democracy and Education.*

3. Values are as unstable as the forms of clouds.—*Experience and Nature.*

4. There is no value except where there is satisfaction, but there have to be certain conditions fulfilled to transform a satis-

faction into a value. . . . Values may be connected inherently with liking, and yet not with every liking but only with those that judgment has approved.—*The Quest for Certainty*.

5. I hold that enjoyments, objects of desires as they arise, are *not* values, but are problematic material for construction—for creation if you will—of values.—A Reply in *The Philosophy of John Dewey* (a Symposium, ed. by P. A. Schilpp).

6. Values that are "extrinsic" or instrumental may be rationally estimated. For they are only means; are not ends in any genuine sense. As means their efficacy may be determined by methods that will stand scientific inspection. But the "ends" they serve (ends which are truly ends) are just matters of what groups, classes, sects, races, or whatever, happen irrationally to like or dislike.—*Problems of Men*.

See also: Criticism; Culture 1; Democracy 8; Faith 1; God; Labor; Philosophy 2; Possibility 2; Religion 8; Responsibility 4; Society 3.

W

WAR

1. Like Greek slavery or feudal serfdom, war and the existing economic regime are social patterns woven out of the stuff of instinctive activities. Native human nature supplies the raw materials, but custom furnishes the machinery and the designs. ... Pugnacity, rivalry, vainglory, love of booty, fear, suspicion, anger, desire for freedom from the conventions and restrictions of peace, love of power and hatred of oppression, opportunity for novel displays, love of home and soil, attachment to one's people and to the altar and the hearth, courage, loyalty, opportunity to make a name, money or a career, affection, piety to ancestors and ancestral gods—all of these things and many more make up the war-like force. To suppose there is some one unchanging native force which generates war is as naive as the usual assumption that our enemy is actuated solely by the meaner of the tendencies named and we only by the nobler. —*Human Nature and Conduct.*

2. Men justify war in behalf of words which would be empty were they not charged with emotional force—words like honor, liberty, civilization, divine purpose and destiny—forgetting that a war, like anything else, has specific concrete results on earth. Unless war can be shown to be the most economical method of

securing the results which are desirable with a minimum of the undesirable results, it marks waste and loss; it must be adjudged a violence, not a use of force. The terms, honor, liberty, future of civilization, justice, become sentimental phantasies of the same order as the catchwords of the professional pacifist. Their emotional force may keep men going, but they throw no light on the goal or on the way traveled.—*Characters and Events.*

3. Treaties to make war have, it would seem, an irresistibly attractive and binding force; treaties not to make war are in all probability scraps of paper.—*Ibid.,* II.

4. I am not convinced beyond every peradventure of a doubt that the outlawry of war will rid the world finally of the war system. If nations insist upon fighting they will do so, just as individuals commit suicide.—*Are Sanctions Necessary to International Organization?* (a Pamphlet).

5. War is as much a social pattern as is the domestic slavery which the ancients thought to be an immutable fact.—*Problems of Men.*

See also: Human Nature; Interaction 4; Peace; Power 2.

WISDOM

1. Wisdom . . . is the nurse of all the virtues.—*Ethics* (with J. H. Tufts).

2. Wisdom differs from knowledge in being the application of what is known to intelligent conduct of the affairs of human life.—*Problems of Men.*

See also: Good and Evil 3.

WORDS

1. A word is an instrument for thinking about the meaning which it expresses.—*How We Think.*

2. Words, the counters for ideas, are easily taken for ideas. —*Democracy and Education.*

3. A word means one thing in relation to a religious institution, still another thing in business, a third thing in law, and so on. This fact is the real Babel of communication.—*Logic: the Theory of Inquiry.*

4. We say that words are a means of communicating ideas. But upon some subjects . . . the words at our disposal are largely such as to prevent the communication of ideas. The words are so loaded with associations derived from a long past that instead of being tools for thought, our thoughts become subservient tools of words. The meanings of such words as soul, mind, self, unity, even body, are hardly more than condensed epitomes of mankind's age-long efforts at interpretation of its experience. These efforts began when man first emerged from the state of the anthropoid ape. The interpretations which are embodied in the words that have come down to us are the products of desire and hope, of chance circumstance and ignorance, of the authority exercised by medicine men and priests as well as of acute observation and sound judgment.—In *Intelligence in the Modern World* (ed. by J. Ratner).

See also: Language 4; War 2.

WORK

1. It is "natural" for activity to be agreeable. It tends to find fulfillment, and finding an outlet is itself satisfactory, for it marks partial accomplishment. If productive activity has become so inherently unsatisfactory that men have to be artificially induced to engage in it, this fact is ample proof that the conditions under which work is carried on balk the complex of activities instead of promoting them, irritate and frustrate natural tendencies instead of carrying them forward to fruition. Work then becomes labor, the consequence of some aboriginal

curse which forces man to do what he would not do if he could help it, the outcome of some original sin which excluded man from a paradise in which desire was satisfied without industry, compelling him to pay for the means of livelihood with the sweat of his brow. From which it follows naturally that Paradise Regained means the accumulation of investments such that a man can live upon their return without labor. There is, we repeat, too much truth in this picture. But it is not a truth concerning original human nature and activity. It concerns the form human impulses have taken under the influence of a specific social environment. If there are difficulties in the way of social alteration—as there certainly are—they do not lie in an original aversion of human nature to serviceable action, but in the historic conditions which have differentiated the work of the laborer for wage from that of the artist, adventurer, sportsman, soldier, administrator and speculator.—*Human Nature and Conduct*.

2. Work has been onerous, toilsome, associated with a primeval curse. It has been done under compulsion and the pressure of necessity, while intellectual activity is associated with leisure. On account of the unpleasantness of practical activity, as much of it as possible has been put upon slaves and serfs. Thus the social dishonor in which this class was held was extended to the work they do.—*The Quest for Certainty*.

See also: Ideals 1; Labor; Leisure; Machine 1; Production and Consumption 2; School 1.

WORLD

1. We live in a world which is an impressive and irresistible mixture of sufficiencies, tight completenesses, order, recurrences which make possible prediction and control, and singularities, ambiguities, uncertain possibilities, processes going on to consequences as yet indeterminate.—*Experience and Nature*.

2. Through science we have secured a degree of power of prediction and of control; through tools, machinery and an accompanying technique we have made the world more conformable to our needs, a more secure abode. We have heaped up riches and means of comfort between ourselves and the risks of the world. We have professionalized amusement as an agency of escape and forgetfulness. But when all is said and done, the fundamentally hazardous character of the world is not seriously modified, much less eliminated.—*Ibid.*

3. There is, of course, a natural world that exists independently of the organism, but this world is environment only as it enters directly and indirectly into life-functions.—*Logic: the Theory of Inquiry.*

See also: Experience 7; Law of Nature 3; Mathematics 3; Mind 5; Self 4; Universe 2.

Y

YOUTH

1. The development within the young of the attitudes and dispositions necessary to the continuous and progressive life of a society cannot take place by direct conveyance of beliefs, emotions, and knowledge. It takes place through the intermediary of the environment.—*The School and Society.*

2. When customs are flexible and youth is educated as youth and not as premature adulthood, no nation grows old.—*Human Nature and Conduct.*

See also: Education 7, 8; Teaching 5.